TEXTILES
IN TRANSITION

Recent Titles in
Contributions in Economics and Economic History
Series Editor: Robert Sobel

TEXTILES IN TRANSITION

Technology, Wages, and Industry Relocation in the U.S. Textile Industry, 1880–1930

Nancy Frances Kane

CONTRIBUTIONS IN ECONOMICS AND ECONOMIC HISTORY, NUMBER 79
GREENWOOD PRESS
NEW YORK · WESTPORT, CONNECTICUT · LONDON

Library of Congress Cataloging-in-Publication Data

Kane, Nancy Frances, 1954–
  Textiles in transition : technology, wages, and industry
relocation in the U.S. textile industry, 1880–1930 / Nancy Frances Kane.
    p.   cm.—(Contributions in economics and economic history,
ISSN 0084–9235 ; no. 79)
  Bibliography: p.
  Includes index.
  ISBN 0–313–25529–6 (lib. bdg. : alk. paper)
  1. Cotton textile industry—United States—History.   I. Title.
II. Series.
HD9875.K3   1988
338.4'767721'097—dc19   87–24950

British Library Cataloguing in Publication Data is available.

Library of Congress Catalog Card Number: 87–24950
ISBN: 0–313–25529–6
ISSN: 0084–9235

First published in 1988

Greenwood Press, Inc.
88 Post Road West, Westport, Connecticut 06881

Printed in the United States of America

The paper used in this book complies with the
Permanent Paper Standard issued by the National
Information Standards Organization (Z39.48–1984).

10 9 8 7 6 5 4 3 2 1

Contents

Tables and Figure

TABLES

Acknowledgments

I am grateful to Professors Edward E. Leamer and Kenneth L. Sokoloff at the University of California at Los Angeles for their guidance in this work. Special thanks to Lee E. Ohanian for numerous valuable comments and suggestions. Responsibility for any errors or omissions remains my own.

TEXTILES
IN TRANSITION

1

Introduction

The U.S. cotton textile industry, one of the earliest American manufacturing pursuits, has weathered many changes in its almost two-hundred-year existence. Throughout this period, rapid and continuous technological advances in textile machinery have allowed U.S. mills to take great strides in increasing productivity and to remain competitive with foreign producers. Textile production has evolved from labor-intensive methods in the days of the hand loom to highly automated manufacturing in today's mills, and robots have begun to replace human labor in many tasks.

Along with the transformation in textile manufacturing technology, the industry withstood a dramatic shift in the location of domestic production. The cotton textile industry underwent an almost complete, although prolonged, relocation between 1880 and 1930, as the center of production shifted from the Northeast to the South in that fifty-year period. This study explores the factors that attracted textile production to the southern states and led to the long duration of the relocation. The role played by technological changes in textile production in promoting this relocation is highlighted in this work.

Low wages drew the textile industry to the southern states after 1880 and are thought to have been the primary advantage held by mills in the South during the period of competition with northern textile mills. The pattern of changes in regional wages and the convergence in the regional wage differential in this period are documented in this study. Explanations for the existence of the low-wage advantage in the South in the late nineteenth century and for the subsequent narrowing of the wage gap between the North and the South are explored in depth.

The relocation of the American textile industry has received much attention from economic historians. This study contributes to that literature by offering a new perspective on changes in the industry based on data from textile mill directories that were published in that period. The Davison's Textile Blue Book and the Official American Textile Directory provide a comprehensive survey of the mills operating in various segments of the industry. This research based on evidence from the textile directories provides fresh information about the individual mills that operated in each region before 1930 to afford new insight into the study of the textile industry relocation.

Textile mill directories are a source of vital details about virtually every mill operating in the United States since the 1860s. Information about individual mills is particularly important for research on the southern textile industry, since southern mill records are rare. A number of northern mill records exist, however, and have been collected by the Baker Library at the Harvard Business School. Nevertheless, a comprehensive set of data about all the northern mills operating before 1930 contributes to the existing knowledge of the northern industry.

The mill directories published information about the cotton textile mills annually. Descriptions of each mill were capsulized in the directory under the name of the mill, arranged by state and mill town. The directory information is first used to collect data about the industry in each region. Changes in the regional industry are analyzed by comparing statistics about the mills operating in each region between 1880 and 1930. Next, the operation of individual mills is tracked during that period to discover which mills survived in each region. Surviving mills are then compared to the mills that failed before 1930 to discover what factors led to mill survival.

The study of the textile industry on such a detailed level will provide insights into how the northern branch of the industry managed to thrive into the 1920s, despite an apparent low-wage advantage in the South. Regional differences in mill survival will also suggest how the economic environment varied between the North and the South in this period and can shed light on why it took so long for the relocation to be completed.

Economic historians have suggested three possible explanations for the curiously long duration of the relocation. The hypotheses focus on factors that may have hindered the textile industry in the South, namely, the inadequate supply of skilled workers in the South, the underdevelopment of the southern capital markets, and the timing of technological advances in textile machinery that allowed the substitution of unskilled for skilled labor in textile production.

Among the three potential factors, labor, capital, or technology, the directory data are most relevant to the issue of technological changes in the industry. The mill descriptions provide details about the type of equipment used in the mills, differentiating between older models of spindles and the newer, advanced types. On the basis of the information about the spindles used in the mills, the role of technological change in the growth of the textile industry in each region is investigated. Information about mill capital and employment sheds light on the competing hypotheses.

DIRECTORY DATA

Data describing cotton textile mills were collected from the Davison's Textile Blue Books, published annually by the Davison Publishing Company, and from the annual Official American Textile Directory. The mill directories first classified mills into different textile segments, and then listed mills by city in each state. All the cotton textile mills operating in Massachusetts and North Carolina were chosen for this study, since each state had the largest number of mills of the textile states in the North and South. The cotton textile segment is defined in this study as those mills producing cotton yarn or cotton fabrics, but excludes mills producing small cotton wares (thread or cordage), elastic, cotton waste, or mattresses.

Mill information was recorded at five-year intervals, beginning in 1885 and concluding with the 1930 directory. Davison's directories were the primary source for information and were supplemented by the Official American Textile directories. The total number of mills included over the entire forty-five-year period was 350 in Massachusetts and 683 in North Carolina. Each mill was listed by name, along with information about the location of the mill, names of upper management, type of output, value of mill capital, number of employees and equipment, type of power used, and the name and population of the city in which the mill was located. The directories appear to be designed for traveling equipment salesmen, since the listings are organized at the local level and the books are full of equipment advertisements.

As with any historical data source, there are deficiencies in the directories. Some of the mill listings are incomplete and report only a part of the items usually included in the entries. The directories did not begin reporting the type of spindles used until the early–twentieth-century issues, and even then the reporting was somewhat sporadic. Mills did not always indicate what grade of yarn was produced and sometimes omitted information about capital or labor. The Official American Textile Directory was often used to complete such entries. This problem with incomplete data justifies choosing to study those states with the greatest mill density in each region, to ensure the maximum number of useful mill listings.

Previous studies have used the mill directories, but to a lesser extent than this work. Mary Oates (1975) based her study of the southern textile industry in the period 1900 to 1940 on data from the Davison's Textile Blue Books. The mill data were aggregated to the county level in her study, however, which obscured the information about individual mills. Oates investigated the number of mills, number of spindles and employees, and type of yarn or cloth produced in over two hundred counties in the Piedmont region of the South to quantify the extent of textile production in each county, using the Davison's directory information. Profiles of the textile industry in each county were used to analyze the relationship between textile production and economic development in the county. Oates' results challenge the assumption that the introduction of the textile industry in the South promoted economic growth.

The present study makes different use of the Davison's Blue Books in several ways. Oates' work focused on the development of the South, whereas this study investigates the relocation of the industry and includes information about both northern and southern mills listed in the directories. In addition, the present study uses a wider range of information available from the directories than did the earlier study. The issues investigated in the two studies are quite distinct and naturally lead to different use of the same data sources.

The other major work that used directory data is a study of the textile industry in Fall River, Massachusetts by T. R. Smith (1944). Smith compiled information from the Davison's directory about mills operating in Fall River in the 1920s to investigate why mills failed in that period. To test the role of the type of cloth produced in determining mill survival, Smith used the directories to identify each mill's product and its fate in the 1920s. Liquidation was often reported in the directory the year the mill closed and could otherwise be determined by the mill's disappearance from subsequent directories. Smith classified Fall River mills operating in 1925 by the type of cloth produced and further divided mills into survivors and those that subsequently failed, to determine if the survival rate varied across product categories.

This study builds on Smith's approach by using the directories as a tool for identifying mills that failed before 1930 and to describe characteristics that might distinguish them from surviving mills. The present research expands that approach to encompass a broader sample of northern mills and to introduce southern mills into the analysis. Moreover, a wider range of mill characteristics, in addition to the type of cloth produced, is considered.

PLAN OF STUDY

This study begins in Chapter 2 with a review of the competing hypotheses about the reasons for the prolonged pace of the relocation of the textile industry to the South. This summary of literature that has addressed the factors leading to relocation is rich in historical detail of the industry in this period, which provides a foundation for the discussion that follows.

Evidence from the mill directories, supplemented with census data, is evaluated in Chapters 3 through 6. A profile of the mills operating in each region based on information from mill directories between 1885 and 1930 is presented in Chapter 3, along with regional information provided by the Census of Manufactures. Adoption of technological changes in textile production is investigated in Chapter 4, where the switch from mule spinning to ring spinning in the late nineteenth century is analyzed.

Chapters 5 and 6 present a detailed study of the mills that survived in each region through 1930. In Chapter 5 a statistical comparison of surviving and nonsurviving mills is made to suggest distinguishing factors that may have contributed to mill failures and to the collapse of the industry in the North in the 1920s. Chapter 6 proceeds with regression analysis of the probability of mill survival and growth of mill capacity, two indicators of industry expansion in a region.

The hypotheses about the constraints surrounding the relocation process are reconsidered in Chapter 7 in light of the information gathered from the mill directories. New evidence from the directories about the rate of adoption of technological changes in spindle machinery is particularly relevant to questions concerning the role of technological change in the relocation of the textile industry.

Textile wages in each region and the tendency toward wage equalization between the North and the South in this period are discussed in Chapter 8. Theories about the source of the interregional wage differential and the subsequent convergence in regional wages are reviewed. This study contributes to the debate by introducing a new perspective based on international trade theory to explain the pattern of changes in interregional textile wage differentials.

Chapter 9 examines the evolution of the American textile industry and the pressures faced by domestic mills with the ongoing relocation of the industry to low-wage regions. The similarities between the current U.S. struggle and the experience of the northern mills a century earlier are striking. Chapter 10 reviews the contribution of this research to the study of the American textile industry between 1880 and 1930 and draws conclusions about the lessons to be learned from this period.

Appendix A reports the methodology of data collection for this research and the special problems encountered in using the textile directories.

For readers unfamiliar with the manufacture of textile products, Appendix B outlines the stages of textile production and describes the significant technological developments in the industry since 1800.

2

Theories about the Relocation of the Textile Industry

TEXTILE INDUSTRY RELOCATION

The center of U.S. cotton textile production gradually shifted from the Northeast to the South from 1880 to 1930. The relocation is most often attributed to cheap southern wages, which were as low as 50 percent of northern wages in the late nineteenth century. Although there is evidence that the regional wage differential diminished unevenly over the period of relocation, southern wages remained 30 percent lower than northern wages in 1930.[1] Even after accounting for possible regional differences in labor productivity, cost of living, and other factors that could mitigate the impact of the lower southern wages on production costs, southern mills still appear to have enjoyed a low-wage advantage. Regional wage differences are discussed in greater detail in Chapter 8.

Other cost advantages in the South, thought to be less significant, include lower tax rates and cheaper fuel (due to the proximity to coal), but these costs represent a small percentage of total costs (Lemert 1933, 161). The earlier southern mills may have had lower raw cotton input costs because the mills were located near the southern cotton fields. This advantage was soon eliminated, however, as southeastern sources of cotton became inadequate for the increased demand for cotton in general and for better quality cotton, as finer grades of yarn were produced. As mills turned to southwestern cotton, transportation costs to each region were then equalized (Copeland 1912, 36). Cotton prices were determined in the national market, so all mills paid the same market price for raw cotton, regardless of their location.

Several studies of regional textile production costs have found that southern production costs were about 85 percent of northern costs for a given type of cloth, largely due to lower labor costs (Fischbaum 1965, 26). As a result, southern mills were often reported to be more profitable than northern mills. Southern mill profits were thought to be extraordinary in the beginning period of mill construction; "it was not unusual for mills in these years to make 30 per cent to 75 per cent profit" (Mitchell 1921, 265). Numerous late–nineteenth-century sources discussed the relatively higher profits earned in the South (Galenson 1975, Chapter 9).

Economists are intrigued by the dynamics of the U.S. textile industry relocation. Why did the relocation proceed so slowly, over a fifty-year period, in spite of the cost advantages in the South that were apparent early? Northern production continued to grow through 1920, and, although southern mill construction began to expand rapidly after 1880, southern mill capacity and output did not exceed that in the North until the 1920s. The relocation may have been hindered by one or all of the following factors: (1) the scarcity of southern skilled labor, (2) the underdeveloped southern financial capital market, and (3) the pace of technological changes in textile production.

LABOR

Southern textile production may have been constrained by the quality of the mill labor force. Gavin Wright (1981) ties the pattern of the southern takeover of U.S. textile production to the development of a skilled mill-labor force in the South between 1880 and 1930. In his view the fact that the South dominated the northern industry only gradually, along increasing grades of yarn and cloth output, reflects the early limitations of southern mill workers. Wright argues that southern mills could at first compete only in coarse yarns and cloth types, because the southern worker lacked the necessary skills to produce finer yarns. Southern workers were initially adept only at the simplest of jobs, he believes, since the mills drew from a rural population, and most workers had no experience with the factory system or with textile machinery.

Wright finds support for his view based on several contemporary observations that southern mill labor was less productive than workers in the North before 1930. For example, southern mill owners apparently complained about the unreliability of southern workers. A high rate of absenteeism led southern mills to maintain a certain amount of "spare help," as much as 25 percent of the mill's normal labor force (Kohn 1907, 61). In addition, recent estimates of the productivity of labor in each region between 1879 and 1919 reveal lower productivity among southern mill workers than in the North (Galenson 1975, 169). Alice Galenson shows, moreover, that the regional differences in productivity narrowed over time, which suggests that southern labor quality did improve as production expanded in that region.

Evidence from census labor surveys reveals that the southern mill workers' characteristics changed over time in a way that may imply improvements in their labor productivity. Wright holds that the demographic development of the southern mill labor force is consistent with a process of "learning-by-doing" that would have raised southern labor productivity. Using age as a proxy for experience and skill, Wright compares the age and sex composition of each region's mill labor force. Initially, the southern labor force had a larger share of younger and female workers than in the North. By 1920, however, the profile of the labor force had become very similar to the northern mill workers. In 1920 the majority of the mill labor in both regions was male, and the regional labor forces had comparable age distributions (Wright 1981, 611). The maturation of the southern labor force implied productivity growth among workers, since age and wages were positively associated (assuming that wages and productivity are correlated). Wright presents evidence from a 1907 census report that shows how earnings per hour rose the older the textile worker that year (1981, 609). In particular, earnings were higher for older workers in the same job category (1981, 610).

The shift in southern cloth specialization to higher grades as the industry expanded in the South may be associated with the accumulation of labor experience, Wright explains. He demonstrates that a higher yarn count required more machine time and greater attention by the spinner to thread breaks, since the yarn became more fragile the thinner it was pulled. In a cross-section study of southern mills operating in 1902, Wright finds that yarn count was positively related to spindle-time per worker, and that yarn output per worker was inversely related to yarn count and positively related to spindle-time per worker (1981, 613).

Following Wright's hypothesis, Leonard Carlson (1981) finds evidence in support of the role played by labor experience in the development of the southern textile industry. Carlson's research suggests that the location of mills in the South was based on the availability of more experienced southern textile workers in certain areas. He argues that southern mills were built in the Piedmont region of the South before 1900, because most experienced southern workers lived there rather than in other southern areas after 1870.

Carlson tested the association between growth in the number of spindles each decade and the total textile industry employment at the beginning of the decade in each state between 1870 and 1900. In addition, his model tested the importance of the state per-capita income, which reflected the level of wages in each state. His results showed a strong positive correlation between growth in a state's textile production capacity, measured by spindles, and the initial level of textile employment in that state. In addition, spindle growth was inversely related to per-capita income (a proxy for wages) each decade. Carlson notes that the relative importance of employment compared to wages seemed to be higher in the earlier decades, whereas wages played a larger role in later decades (1981, 67).

Carlson also examines the relationship between mill location and grade of textile output. He finds that mills producing high count yarns, which he defines as medium and fine grades, were concentrated in the established textile states, closer to sources of the more experienced southern workers. Medium and fine grades are assumed to require skilled workers, since production becomes more difficult as the grade of yarn spun increases. An association between the proportion of medium and fine grade output and the employment in textiles in each state was found for data including ten southern states in 1900. Carlson also finds a positive relationship between average count of each state's production and employment (1981, 69).

Although the alleged deficiency of southern labor in this period is a controversial point that warrants a look at opposing views, a fuller discussion of those arguments is postponed to Chapter 7.

CAPITAL

Another possible restraint on the relocation of the textile industry may have been an insufficient supply of capital for financing the building of mills in the South. Although the scarcity of local capital could have been remedied by an inflow of capital from other regions, Lance Davis (1971) argues that barriers to capital mobility hindered the interregional flow of financial capital from the North to the capital-scarce South. Moreover, the extent of interregional capital mobility was critical to the pace of industrialization in the South, he believes. "It was the second decade of the twentieth century before southern textiles clearly dominated the American market: a domination they would almost certainly have achieved a hundred years earlier had capital been more mobile" (1971, 293).

Davis points to the persistence of interest-rate differentials between the South and other regions for evidence of barriers to capital mobility in that region. In his view high southern interest rates would have induced capital inflows from the North, resulting in a reduction in southern rates, had capital been more mobile. In his study of the evolution of a national capital market in the period 1869 to 1914, Davis (1965) found that interregional interest-rate differentials, measured by net returns on earning assets of rural banks, existed between capital-scarce regions and the capital-abundant North. Those interest-rate differentials narrowed substantially over the period in most regions, which Davis attributes to the development of a national capital market. The South stood alone as a special case, however. While interest rates in other regions tended toward convergence, southern interest rates remained high relative to other U.S. regions. Subsequent studies have corroborated this pattern of regional interest-rate movements, although methods of constructing interest-rate series have varied (Smiley 1975, James 1978).

The existence of interregional interest-rate differentials and the process of capital market integration that led to a narrowing of those differentials in areas other than the South may be explained by several alternative hypotheses. Interest-rate differentials might exist in both perfect and imperfect capital markets. In a perfect capital market, the differential may reflect real costs involved in interregional lending, including transactions and information costs (Stigler 1968, 119). A decline in information costs, due to technological improvements in transportation and communication, could explain the narrowing of interest-rate differentials.

The differential could also reflect differences in risk, even in a perfect capital market. High-interest-rate regions might have had higher rates of default on loans or greater uncertainty about credit risk, due to a shorter credit history among borrowers in the relatively newer regions. The decline in differentials might reflect a lowering of the risk premium earned in the high-interest-rate areas. Davis (1965) has argued that the interest-rate differentials were too large to be explained by risk premiums, however. Nevertheless, risk and information costs likely contributed to part of the interregional interest-rate differences.

A second set of theories about the development of a national capital market is based on the assumption of imperfect capital markets, in which financial intermediaries could earn monopoly rents. In that case higher interest rates in capital-scarce regions are explained by monopoly returns enjoyed by lenders in local markets. Barriers to capital mobility protected local monopoly power, in this view. Economists have investigated a range of possible barriers that might have created imperfect capital markets. Richard Sylla (1969) and John A. James (1978) suggest that legal barriers are to blame, whereas Davis (1965) points to institutional factors.

Sylla argues that federal policy protected national banks from competition in local markets, which gave those institutions local monopoly power, especially in rural areas. The National Banking System, established in 1863, set minimum capital requirements that precluded small agricultural banks from a national charter and prohibited national banks from using real estate as collateral. As a result only 100 of the country's 1,600 national banks were located in the rural South in 1870. Sylla hypothesizes that the convergence in interregional interest rates was due to amendments to the National Banking System in 1900, which reduced capital requirements for the formation of national banks in less-populated towns. The growth in national banks in the South after minimum capital requirements were relaxed in 1900 suggests that the original act had imposed effective barriers to entry, Sylla concludes.

James concurs that interest-rate differentials reflected local monopoly, but disagrees with Sylla's focus on national banks. James argues that growth in state rather than national banks led to the erosion of local monopoly power in this period. He points out that state banks outnumbered and grew more rapidly than national banks after 1896. State-bank minimum capital requirements were generally lower than national-bank capital requirements between 1895 and 1910. Thus, growth in state banks might have been encouraged by the more restrictive capital requirements placed on national banks, if the two types of banks were substitutes. Moreover, James found that lower state-bank minimum capital requirements were associated with lower local loan rates. This suggests that state-bank capital requirements formed effective barriers to capital mobility. Growth in state banks, stimulated by lower minimum capital requirements, was primarily responsible for the convergence in interregional interest-rate differentials, James concludes.

An alternative source of barriers to capital mobility may have been institutional factors.[2] Davis (1965) attributes the narrowing of interest-rate differentials to institutional developments, primarily in the commercial-paper market. He argues that the spread of a nationwide commercial-paper market between 1870 and 1913 introduced competition in cities where banks had long enjoyed monopoly power in their local markets. As a result, loan rates fell as barriers to mobility of short-term capital were overcome.

These forces may have only limited ability to explain interest-rate patterns in the South, however, because this region remained isolated from the evolution of a national capital market in the early–twentieth century. Stressing institutional factors, Davis has pointed to the poor representation by all types of financial institutions in the South in this period. The commercial-paper market, to which Davis attributes the development of the national capital market, failed to develop in the South. Commercial banking grew slowly in the South, and the region was slow to participate in free banking. The banks that were established serviced the commercial sector, rather than industry and agriculture, and enjoyed local monopoly power. Mutual savings banks, mortgage companies, and life insurance companies were not important in the South in this period.

Davis suggests several possible explanations for the slower development of financial institutions in the South. The Civil War destroyed financial connections between the North and the South, which could not be immediately repaired. Also, the fact that southern states were not represented in Congress when the National Banking System was designed in 1863 explains why the provisions of the system failed to suit the needs of the South. Southerners may have been resistant to dealing with paper issues in the financial markets, following bad experiences with Confederate bonds during the war. The social and political ties to agriculture may have impeded the flow of capital to manufacturing in the South and may have created an obstacle to the inflow of northern capital and investment.

James also addresses the issue of the persistence of southern interest-rate differentials relative to the rest of the country. He argues that the population structure of the rural South allowed country banks to exert monopoly power for a longer period than in more densely populated regions. The widely dispersed population did not support a sufficient number of competing banks to erode local monopoly power. By implication, the process of urbanization of the South, which lagged behind that of the rest of the nation, eventually reduced the territorial monopoly that banks could enjoy in that region.

For a number of reasons, then, capital-market integration was slow to evolve in the South. Southern mills likely were hindered by a scarcity both of traditional sources of capital for funding the growth of existing mills, and of risk capital for investment in new ventures. Financing for the development of new firms and industries, now known as venture capital, involves specialized services from financial intermediaries. Since the risk of business failure is greater during the early stages of the business than at any other time during its life cycle, lending to a new or young company involves greater credit risk than lending to an established business. Southern bankers, unfamiliar with lending to the industrial sector, probably were wary of participating in venture-capital projects.

Venture-capital resources are an important requirement for the introduction of a new industry in a region, since traditional sources of funds may not be channeled to developing enterprises unless lenders are experienced in risky venture-capital financing. John Hekman and John S. Strong (1981) argue that New England's venture-capital resources have played an important role in that region's industrial evolution by helping new industries get started. Moreover, the scarcity of venture capital in other regions, especially the South, has inhibited industrial development. As a result, industrialization has tended to originate in the favorable environment of New England, from cotton textiles early in the nineteenth century to computers today.

The early northern venture-capital market was funded by wealthy individuals and merchant capital. Family wealth was an important source of funding for many early enterprises, and family ties could facilitate lending by creditors.[3] Mercantile profits were directed toward industry and transportation after the War of 1812 constricted trade, and early mill centers and northern canal projects were backed by merchant capital. New England merchants were experienced with managing high-risk investments in the overseas trade business and could transfer their skills to venture-capital activities in the emerging northern manufacturing industries.

The domestic venture-capital market apparently remains fragmented. Hekman and Strong believe that a well-developed national venture-capital market still has not evolved. New England remains a lending center of risk finance, because of the financial sector's experience with venture-capital projects. "The region's banks and financial institutions have become more active in and inclined toward venture capital finance. . . . In addition, the financial institutions of New England appear to be more venture-capital oriented than those in other regions" (Hekman and Strong 1981, 45). In addition to the delayed growth of financial intermediation in the South, the lack of experience with high-risk finance in the southern capital markets may have further hindered the growth of the textile industry in that region.

Some interregional transfer of capital to the southern textile industry did occur, however, by circumventing the underdeveloped capital market in the South. Mills could obtain funds directly from northern sources, thus bypassing the region's financial institutions. Working capital was provided by the northern firms that did business with the southern mills, primarily northern machine companies and commission houses.

Northern machine companies extended credit on machine purchases, and southern mills relied on longer credit terms than northern mills. In his history of the Whitin Machine Works, Thomas Navin reports that "whereas in the North over 80 percent of all bills were collected within six months after presentation, in the South only about 30 percent were collected within that period and about 20 percent were allowed to ride for two years or more" (1950, 227). Moreover, southern mills were charged an additional percentage point interest on the balance owed for the machinery compared to northern mills (1950, 227). The higher finance charges for southern mills could reflect both higher market rates of interest in the South as well as higher credit risk compared to northern mills, which were probably more familiar to the machine companies.

Northern commission houses provided financial assistance to the southern mills on an ongoing basis, in return for the exclusive right to market a mill's products. Commission houses extended credit, accepted mill stock as payment, and endorsed bank notes for the southern mills (Copeland 1912, 210). By aiding a mill that was strapped for working capital, a commission house could establish a long-term relationship with a producer and secure a dependable source of cotton goods for marketing. The selling agent could also monitor the type, quality, and price of a mill's products by backing the mill's operations (Navin 1950, 228).

Commission houses, like the machine companies, charged a premium for lending to southern firms. T. W. Uttley reported in his 1904 account of U.S. cotton textile mills that the southern mills, lacking working capital, borrowed "at a high rate of interest from a commission house" (1905, 46). Melvin Copeland estimates that the commission houses required a 2 percent premium for handling southern goods, to compensate for the higher risk in dealing with southern mills. According to Copeland, the risk premium reflects both the inferiority of the southern product and the higher credit risk of southern mills, "which are generally smaller, less strong financially, and too remote to be easily watched" (1912, 210).

Of the two northern businesses, commission houses were probably the more important source of working capital. Northern machine companies also bought mill stock, but were less likely than the commission houses to hold mill stock and usually sold it as soon as possible. Since machine companies typically dealt with a mill only when a plant was initially equipped or when machinery was replaced or serviced, machine builders had less reason to take an active role in promoting a mill by investing in stock.

The practice of accepting stock varied widely among machine companies, ranging from the Lowell Machine Shop's policy (up to 1905) of never taking stock, to some taking stock from only well-established mills, while others accepted stock from most customers. In the late nineteenth century some machine companies apparently were reluctant to accept mill stock in partial payment because inter-corporate stock transactions were thought to be illegal under common law, until the practice became generally accepted in the 1890s (Navin 1950, 231). Machine companies sometimes contributed a large part of a new mill's capital base, however, and in many cases machinery builders were reported to have supplied "up to 20 percent of the capital going into individual mill ventures" (Navin 1950, 230).

Additional northern capital was mobilized via direct investment, as northern textile companies opened southern branches or relocated mills to the South. In addition, northern capitalists had ownership in southern mills. The extent of northern ownership of southern mill stock has not been quantified reliably, however, and reports varied from low to high estimates of dependence on northern capital. Most sources suggest that the South relied primarily on local capital, however. In his 1907 study of the industry in South Carolina, August Kohn notes with confidence that at least 75 percent of all textile capital was owned within that state (1907, 211). Broadus Mitchell concurs that the chief sources of southern mill capital were local (1921, 233).

These writers note that much of the southern mill stock was initially sold to northern machine companies, but that the shares were quickly disposed of by those firms and eventually were held by southern investors. For example, Uttley visited a South Carolina mill where "62 per cent of the stock was originally held by Northern machinists, but that by now it had all come South again and was held to a large extent locally" (1905, 47). The relatively small participation in southern mill stock by northern investors apparently continued throughout this period, as revealed by a 1923 survey of southern mills that estimated only 14 percent of mill capital was owned by Northerners (Lahne 1944, 89). These impressions of the role of local capital in the southern textile industry are supported by more general findings concerning growth of capital stock for the industrial sector in the South in this period. Richard Easterlin (1957, 141–203) estimates that about 75 percent of the growth of southern nonagricultural capital stock was generated by local savings in the period 1880–1921.

Although many writers argue that northern capital played a minor role in the growth of the southern textile industry, this does not contradict Davis' hypothesis that the flow of northern capital to the South would have been greater with lower barriers to interregional capital flows. There are too many accounts of capital scarcity in the South and in southern mills in particular to assume that the opportunities for mill growth were satisfied by local capital sources. A high share of local owner-ship of southern mill stock is not in itself evidence that mill growth was not constrained by the supply of southern capital resources. Indeed, Galenson (1975) emphasizes that while the lack of financial intermediaries in the South was overcome to some extent via direct investment in mill equity, southern cap-ital was nevertheless inadequate for the southern mills' desired rate of growth.

TECHNOLOGICAL CHANGE

Improvements in textile machinery also played a role in the relocation of the textile industry. Hekman (1980) has linked skilled-labor-saving innovations to the movement of the textile industry to the unskilled-labor-abundant South. The introduc-tion of automatic machinery that could be tended by unskilled workers made it possible for mills to open in the South, despite the deficiency in an experienced mill labor force. Technological change in textiles "facilitated the rapid development of the South's textile industry after 1880 by replacing operations per-formed by skilled labor with automatic machinery" (1980, 711). Also, the standardization of the machinery reduced the neces-sity for the mill to be located near the machine producers, who remained concentrated in the North.

Hekman draws on the "product cycle" theory developed by Raymond Vernon (1966). The product cycle describes phases of the production process for a particular good, in which a prod-uct moves from early to mature stages of development. Typi-cally, in early stages of the production process, firms rely on specialized suppliers and skilled labor. When a product is first introduced the production process undergoes constant changes as techniques and machinery are perfected and technological innovations are introduced. Creative managerial and mechani-cal skills are necessary to form the new product. Later in the product cycle, the market for the product grows to support mass production, and the production process becomes standardized. Automation is introduced in the mature stages of production, once a minimum scale of output is warranted. Hekman traces the product cycle of cotton textiles from the early stages requiring the specialized inputs that were available in the North to the start of the mature stage of the cycle that led to the relocation of the industry to the South.

Although Hekman and Wright agree that the southern mill labor force was unskilled in the late nineteenth century, Hekman's hypothesis does not depend on any change in the quality of the southern worker. Hekman argues that the upgrading of southern textile output through 1930 was facilitated by the gradual improvements in the machinery that became adapted to the production of finer grades of yarn and cloth. Unskilled labor was capable of operating the various new models of textile machinery throughout the period, so an increase in the quality of the southern mill labor force was not necessary for the industry relocation to proceed.

The two inventions that had the greatest impact on textile production were the ring spindle and the Northrop automatic loom. Both replaced skilled operators with automatic machinery and increased the number of machines operated per worker. The labor-saving feature came at a price, however; the new machines cost generally three times the price of the traditional models. For example, prices for automatic looms ranged from $130 to $170 per loom, compared to $40 to $60 for comparable-width standard looms in the early twentieth century (Feller 1966, 335).

The ring spindle was invented in the United States in 1831, but was not widely adopted until the 1870s, after further improvements in its design were made. As an indication of the attention devoted to perfecting the spindle, no less than 373 patents were taken out on the ring spindles between 1870 and 1903 (Copeland 1909, 127). The ring was initially suited to replace the mule spindle in the spinning of coarse yarns only. The mule spindle continued to be used throughout the period, however, primarily in the production of fine yarn. The ring spindle had the advantage of operating at a higher speed and requiring less strength and skill from the operator. In addition to the production of more output per worker, the ring allowed the substitution of low-wage labor for the high-wage mule spinner.[4] Women and children were suited to work on the ring, because only the piecing of broken threads was involved in tending the spindle, a relatively easy and unskilled task. In contrast, since the mule was operated by pushing the heavy machinery back and forth, the mule spinner was usually a man.

The Northrop automatic loom, first marketed by the Draper Company in 1894, automatically replaced empty bobbins in the shuttle while running continuously. A weaver could tend more looms because he no longer had to stop the loom and refill the bobbin by hand. Since there was less stop time, more output per hour was produced by each loom. An automatic stop motion worked in the event of a broken thread, thus reducing the skill required of the weaver, who no longer had to watch the loom as carefully. The Northrop loom was at first suited to only ring-spun yarn, plain weaves, and narrow widths, but these limitations were eliminated with further improvements.

Southern mills relied on these labor-saving innovations to a greater extent than northern mills. Census data show that ring spindles constituted over 90 percent of all southern spindles as early as 1890, while northern mills reported only about a 60 percent share that year. Ring spindles continued to dominate total spindle capacity in both regions but remained a higher proportion of total spindles in the South throughout this period (see Table 2.1). The reasons for regional differences in the experience with the ring spindle are explored in Chapter 4. Table 2.1 shows that automatic looms also were adopted to a greater extent, in terms of share of total looms, in the South compared to the North.

In addition to the advantage of labor-saving mahinery, the South was noted for its generally more modern, newer equipment. In his tour of the southern mills in 1903 to 1904, Uttley learned that "the present-day mills of the South will compare most favourable with Northern factories, and, as a whole, have probably more modern equipments" (1905, 44). Although southern mills equipped mills with secondhand machinery from the North in the earliest period of southern mill-building, "it was quickly learned that old equipment was a bad bargain at any price" and, as a result, "Southern mills with new machinery throughout. . . . had an advantage over Northern mills that contributed to profits" (Mitchell 1921, 246). Considering

Table 2.1

Composition of Textile Machinery

Ring Spindles (as Share of Total Spindles)			Automatic Looms (as Share of Total Looms)		
Year	Northeast	South	Year	Northeast	South
1890	.59	.93	1890	--	--
1899	.65	.96	1899	.046	.114
1904	.70	.97	1904	.142	.306
1909	.76	.98	1909	.222	.431
1914	.82	.99	1914	.396	.517
1919	--	--	1919	.385	.715
1929	--	--	1929	.591	.803

Source: Census of Manufactures

the relative age differential between the textile industries in each region, it is not surprising that southern mills operated with newer equipment. Unfortunately, historical sources do not provide information about the breakdown of the age of mill equipment in each region.

Newer equipment that embodied the labor-saving developments in textile technology gave the South an advantage because labor costs were a significant portion of cotton textile production costs. For example, labor costs were about 35 percent of the total costs of print cloth production and were second only to material costs, which formed 55 percent of total costs (Smith 1944, 67). Labor costs were concentrated in the areas of weaving and spinning, which constituted 46 and 19 percent of total print cloth costs (Smith 1944, 101). Thus labor-saving developments in these two stages of textile production had the greatest impact on production costs compared to the improvements in other textile departments in this period.

Of the automatic loom, Copeland says that "it has reduced the labor cost of weaving one half, a fact which is all the more important since the labor cost of weaving constituted one half of the entire labor cost of manufacturing cotton cloth" (1909,

146). Uttley found that the weekly total labor cost of $14 for producing print cloth on an automatic loom in the North compared favorably to $21 on a plain loom in 1903 (1905, 25). Similar calculations based on data from southern mills showed that weaving costs were cut in half with the automatic loom (1905, 67). In 1910 the U.S. Tariff Board reported that weaving costs were reduced by about 2 cents per pound of cloth produced. The labor cost of weaving with the automatic loom was 2.8 cents per pound, compared to 4.6 cents with the plain loom (Feller 1966, 342). The ring spindle also reduced labor costs significantly. Smith calculated that the average cost of spinning among Fall River mills using ring spindles declined to 15 cents per yard from 23 cents per yard with mule spindles (1944, 100).

Lower labor costs with the use of the automatic loom and the ring spindle were offset to some extent by the higher capital costs incurred in purchasing these types of equipment. Depending on the rate of interest and the rate of depreciation used to calculate capital costs, the newer types of equipment were not necessarily more profitable than operating with the standard models. The higher prices of the automatic loom and ring spindle may have deterred adoption of these models by some mills, especially if a mill had operating machinery already in place.

Based on data provided by Uttley's research, Feller shows that the capital costs of installed looms may be low enough to offset the savings in labor costs with the automatic loom, since the fixed costs associated with the installed looms are "sunk" or irrelevant (1966, 1968). As long as the comparison between the old and new models is made under the assumption that both techniques are to be bought or that both are already installed, the new model will produce greater savings in production costs. If the older model is already installed, however, Feller has shown that higher capital costs diminished the gains that might be made by switching to the new model. Feller's calculations suggest that the slower rate of adoption of the automatic loom by northern mills may have been a rational choice based on cost conditions before 1910. By 1910, however, the automatic loom appeared to be preferable to plain looms, even after making the appropriate adjustments for differences in capital costs (1968, 629). In Chapter 4 this argument is extended to the case of choosing between ring and mule spindles.

PLAN FOR EVALUATION OF THE THEORIES

The role of each of the three factors that may have hindered the growth of the southern textile industry will be investigated in Chapters 3 through 6. Textile directories provide information about the capital invested in each mill, the population of mill towns, and the use of ring and mule spindles in both the North and the South. By identifying which of these factors were related to the profitability and survival of mills in each region, the importance of capital, labor, and technological change in the growth of the regional industries can be assessed. The theories about the relocation are evaluated in light of the new findings in Chapter 7.

NOTES

1. Contemporary studies find that regional manufacturing wage differentials have persisted between the South and the rest of the United States (see Chapter 8).

2. Even if capital markets are perfect, institutional factors play a role in promoting capital mobility. For example, financial institutions reduce search costs and transactions costs involved in the transfer of funds from savers to borrowers, by specializing in that activity.

3. Today other sources of venture capital include special departments or subsidiaries of banks and nonbank financial institutions organized specifically for venture-capital projects, insurance companies, pension funds, and, since 1980, venture-capital partnerships.

4. In addition to being the most highly paid mill workers, the predominantly English mule spinners were unionized and therefore more difficult for mill owners to manage.

3

Description of Textile Production by Region

DATA SOURCES

The study of the relocation of the textile industry begins with a description of textile production in the regional centers of the industry. Two sources of information about the industry are used to draw an initial comparison of northern and southern textile production. The first source is the Census of Manufactures, which provides broad regional information about the industry each decade. Although census data are based on statistics filed by the individual firms, that information is aggregated to the state and regional level in the published census reports. For detailed information about each textile firm a second data source is used, the Davison's Textile Blue Book mill directory, supplemented by the Official American Textile Directory. The mill directories contain detailed information about many of the items found in the census reports, but unlike the census, the data are reported for each of the mills individually. In addition, the directories were compiled each year, compared to generally every five years for the census reports.

The Census of Manufactures reports statistics about the cotton textile industry in each state, which can be added to get regional totals. Census data for Maine, Massachusetts, New Hampshire, and Rhode Island are totaled to represent the northern textile industry, and Alabama, Georgia, North Carolina, and South Carolina represent the southern industry in the following discussion. The regional information about total output, machinery, capital, and earnings is examined to compare the size and type of output, production capacity, and return on capital in each region. Much of the discussion of the census data has been treated by other authors, but a review of the major differences between textile production in each region establishes a basis for understanding the findings from the mill directory data.

The textile mill directories are rich in descriptions of individual mills. Data were collected from the directories for cotton textile mills in Massachusetts and North Carolina every five years, starting in 1885 and ending in 1930. The average textile mill for a given region and year can be described by finding the mean values for the various characteristics recorded in these directories. Changes in the average mill over the period 1880 to 1930 in each region suggest how the relocation of the industry proceeded and how the industry developed in each region.

CENSUS OF MANUFACTURES

The year 1880 is an appropriate starting date for a comparison of the regional textile data from the Census of Manufactures, because most authors agree that southern textile production did not become significant until then (although there were some mills in operation in the South before 1880). Mitchell presents numerous references attesting to the selection of 1880 as the year marking the beginning of mill-building activity in the South (1921, 59–63). In addition, census data of capital, labor, and machinery in the textile industry in the South since 1850 show a dramatic jump in all these categories beginning in 1880. For example, southern spindles increased 65 percent between 1870 and 1880, then tripled by 1890 and again by 1900. The other parameters of textile production in the South had similar growth rates in this period.

One notable feature of the relocation of textile production is the apparent resiliency of the northern industry up to the 1920s. The value of textile production remained greater in the North than in the South each decade from 1880 to 1920. Evidence that the southern branch dominated the industry did not appear until the 1930 census, when southern output had become twice that of the North (see Table 3.1). Northern output continued to grow at a steady pace through 1920, although at a much slower rate than southern output growth, and output in both regions responded to the extraordinary demand for cotton cloth during World War I. During the following decade, however, northern textile production contracted sharply, while southern output expanded modestly.

Changes in mill capacity mirror changes in output, not surprisingly. Mill capacity is best measured by total spindles (Copeland 1912, 19).[1] Total spindle capacity, total active spindles, and the percentage of inactive spindles are shown by region in Table 3.2. As the result of overcapacity in the industry

Table 3.1
Value of Regional Cotton Textile Output

	Year	Value of Product
North[a]	1880	$130,936,232
	1890	164,788,292
	1900	172,163,837
	1905	204,746,885
	1910	292,308,965
	1915	296,550,659
	1920	894,725,771
	1930	368,672,202
South[b]	1880	$ 13,315,840
	1890	33,590,641
	1900	84,707,498
	1905	148,626,278
	1910	208,858,525
	1915	254,794,419
	1920	818,637,662
	1930	873,623,564

Source: Census of Manufactures
[a] Northern states: Maine, Massachusetts, New Hampshire, Rhode Island
[b] Southern states: Alabama, Georgia, North Carolina, South Carolina

Table 3.2
Active and Inactive Spindles, by Region
(Millions)

Year	South			North		
	Total Spindles	Active Spindles	% Idle	Total Spindles	Active Spindles	% Idle
1906	9.2	9.0	2.2%	14.6	14.4	1.4%
1908	10.5	10.2	2.9	15.5	15.3	1.3
1910	10.9	10.5	3.7	16.0	15.7	1.9
1912	12.0	11.6	3.3	17.6	17.1	2.8
1914	13.0	12.7	2.3	17.7	17.4	1.7
1916	13.5	13.4	0.7	17.8	17.5	1.7
1918	14.5	14.5	0.0	18.3	18.0	1.6
1920	15.2	15.2	0.0	18.5	18.3	1.1
1922	16.1	15.9	1.2	18.9	17.9	5.3
1924	17.2	16.9	1.7	18.6	17.1	8.1
1926	17.9	17.6	1.7	17.9	15.5	13.4
1928	18.5	18.3	1.1	15.5	13.8	11.0
1930	19.1	18.6	2.6	13.5	11.4	15.6

Source: Census of Manufactures

during the 1920s, total U.S. mill capacity began to decline after 1925. The adjustment came entirely from the northern region, however. According to the census data series on spindles reported in each region beginning in 1906, total northern spindles peaked in the early 1920s and then dropped steadily by about one million spindles annually between 1926 and 1932. Total southern spindles continued to expand through the 1920s, although capacity was held constant in the South during the Great Depression.

The sharp rise in inactive spindles in the industry during the 1920s is further evidence that the textile depression hit primarily the northern producers. The proportion of inactive spindles in the South remained quite low through the 1920s, between 1 and 2 percent of total spindles, which was even lower than in previous years in that region. The northern industry experienced a sharp increase in idle capacity, however. The share of northern spindles that were inactive jumped to over 10 percent after 1925 compared with very low rates before the 1920s. Evidence of recession in the North is even more striking when the rising inactive rate is considered in light of the shrinkage in total northern spindle capacity. This suggests that the northern mills could not dispose of idle spindles fast enough to keep up with the erosion of the North's competitive position in the industry in the 1920s.

The Census of Manufactures provides details about the type of output produced by each state, which reveal significant differences between the cotton textile industries in the North and the South. The output of the South was predominantly made up of coarse varieties of cloth and low-count, coarse yarns in the early stages of growth of the southern textile industry.[2] Northern mills produced a wider range of cloth and yarn grades, and a larger share of northern output was graded fine. Regional output composition is summarized in Table 3.3. Over time, output in the finer grades expanded in both regions, and southern output became more similar in composition to the northern output.

The descriptions of regional output show that the southern takeover of total U.S. production proceeded gradually, by grade

Table 3.3
Composition of Regional Output

| | 1890 | | 1900 | | 1910 | | 1920 | | 1930 | |
	N	S	N	S	N	S	N	S	N	S
Sheeting	.21	.31	.13	.27	.14	.27	.24	.28	.10	.21
Print	.20	.03	.24	.09	.29	.24	.07	.12	.04	.15
Drill	.10	.09	.02	.09	.01	.08	.01	.09	.01	.05
Duck	.02	.04	.02	.06	.03	.07	.08	.11	.01	.11
Ticking	.07	.03	.06	.05	.04	.09	.03	.07	.02	.07
Gingham	.06	.13	.04	.08	.07	.06	.04	.05	.01	.02
Fine	.06	.01	.08	.01	.14	.05	--	--	--	--

Source: Census of Manufactures
Note: N = North, S = South

of output, beginning with coarse goods. Although the northern textile industry continued to dominate the production of total U.S. cloth output until the 1920s, the South captured the majority of U.S. production of several categories of cloth output as early as 1900 (see Table 3.4). For example, southern states produced 75 percent of the nation's drill fabrics and exceeded northern production of sheeting and duck fabrics in 1900. Although data on fine output are not available after 1910, since the cloth classifications were redefined in the later reports, the trend toward increased southern production of fine output is suggested by the census data from 1890 to 1910.

The pattern of cloth specialization observed in the census data is best explained by the cost advantages within each region in certain categories of fabrics. David P. Doane (1971) found that the South had a competitive advantage in the production of coarse goods in the late nineteenth century, but that advantage dissipated at higher grades of textile products. In a sample of thirty-eight northern and thirty-two southern mills producing in 1890, the costs of producing sheeting and shirting, which are typical coarse-grade products, were calculated by region. A comparison of average total costs in each region reveals a 10 to

Table 3.4
Regional Output as Share of Total U.S. Output

| | 1890 | | 1900 | | 1910 | | 1920 | | 1930 | |
	N	S	N	S	N	S	N	S	N	S
Sheeting	.68	.23	.45	.47	.34	.46	.43	.46	.19	.78
Print	.85	.03	.78	.16	.57	.32	.37	.58	.12	.88
Drill	.78	.15	.25	.75	.11	.70	.09	.68	.01	.96
Duck	.33	.18	.25	.42	.22	.40	.22	.28	.02	.65
Ticking	.80	.07	.65	.28	.34	.48	.26	.57	.11	.87
Gingham	.48	.27	.49	.45	.40	.23	.32	.31	--	.85
Fine	.88	.01	.74	.04	.66	.16	--	--	--	--
Total	.68	.15	.57	.29	.49	.33	.42	.39	.31	.63

Source: Census of Manufactures
Note: N = North, S = South

20 percent advantage in the South, primarily due to lower labor and materials costs.

Moreover, Doane's calculations show that the South's advantage in lower materials costs was larger, the heavier (lower count) the cloth produced. His result is based on the lower cost of cotton enjoyed by southern mills, which formed the bulk of the total costs of materials in textile production. Southern mills could take advantage of their location near local cotton markets, where prices were lower than in the North because of savings on transportation costs. In 1890 the New York cotton price was 6 percent higher than in the New Orleans market, largely reflecting transport costs. This cost advantage was later eliminated after local cotton supplies became insufficient for the southern mills' consumption of raw cotton because of the rapid growth in southern production. Southern mills then purchased cotton from more distant sources and incurred transport costs that were similar to those paid by northern mills. Lower labor costs probably became the primary source of the southern cost advantage at that point, once cotton prices equalized between the two regions.

The census data appear to refute the claim by some scholars that each region specialized completely in certain segments of the textile industry and did not compete directly in common cotton textile markets. Some historians have argued that the North produced primarily medium and fine grades of cotton products, while the South specialized in coarse goods. Evidence suggests that the competition between the regions was direct, however. Both regions produced goods in most of the categories listed by the census reports. Although northern mills shifted production away from the coarser grades of cotton goods, they did not completely abandon those markets. Also, mills from both regions participated in the national market for textile goods during this period. For example, in an 1892 study of eighty-four U.S. textile firms by the U.S. Commissioner of Labor, a large percentage of both the northern and southern mills in the sample had New York selling agents (Doane 1971, 8). Another indicator of production for a national market is found in a Treasury Department study that reported that most of the textile production by the southern mills was shipped out of state in 1886 (Doane 1971, 8).

One reason that northern mills continued to produce lower grades of textile products, even though the South was thought to have a clear cost advantage in those markets, may be that the northern goods were differentiated in some manner. If northern goods were perceived to be of higher quality than southern, northern mills could have retained some market share of those segments where southern mills were active. Census figures indicate that the value of output per square yard was lower for southern goods than for northern goods of the same type of cloth. This suggests that southern goods received a lower price per yard, perhaps because of inferior quality (Lemert 1933, 86).

Although the issue of mill profits in each region remains controversial, census data point to the possibility that regional profit rates did not begin to diverge significantly until the 1920s. An estimate of net earnings can be calculated from the census reports, because the expenses of textile production were reported (except depreciation) in addition to the value of mill capital.[3] Dividing net earnings by capital stock, the regional rate of return on capital can be estimated and is reported for the period 1890 to 1920 in Table 3.5. Marvin N. Fischbaum (1965) made similar calculations but included more states in his definition of the regions, so his results differ in magnitude and reverse the relative standing of the regional profit rates in some years. This study uses the more commonly accepted definition of the regions by choosing only the significant textile producing states.

Although the southern rate of return is greater than in the North (with the exception of 1910) the differences are very small and range from one to three percentage points. This supports Fischbaum's conclusion that the southern textile advantage did not appear until the 1920s, and that northern mills remained profitable and competitive with the South until then. Comparable profit rates in the two regions are consistent with the finding that the northern textile industry continued to grow, both in quantity of output and production capacity, up to 1920.

These results also cast doubt on the popularly held belief that southern mills enjoyed supernormal profits in the late nine-

Table 3.5
Estimated Regional Return on Capital

	Year	Net Earnings[a] / Capital
North[b]	1890	.075
	1900	.093
	1905	.034
	1910	.113
	1915	.070
	1920	.173
South[c]	1890	.086
	1900	.121
	1905	.049
	1910	.070
	1915	.091
	1920	.187

Source: Calculations by the author based on data from Census of Manufactures

[a] Net earnings calculated as value of product less cost of materials and power, wages, salaries, and miscellaneous expenses; depreciation expense not available.

[b] Northern states: Maine, Massachusetts, New Hampshire, Rhode Island

[c] Southern states: Alabama, Georgia, North Carolina, South Carolina

teenth century. Census data suggest that although southern returns on capital may have been higher than in the North, the difference is small. Early accounts of extreme rates of southern profits in the 1880s and 1890s may have been merely anecdotal or measured inaccurately. Fischbaum suspects that few southern mills allowed for depreciation in that period, which would exaggerate mill earnings and thus inflate reported profit rates in these historical accounts (1965, 46).

There are problems with using the census capital values to measure rates of return, however, especially prior to 1919. The definition of capital varied with each census until 1909 and was abandoned altogether after 1919. Readers were warned of the deficiencies in reported capital in both the 1909 and 1919 censuses of manufactures. In the introduction to the *Fourteenth*

Census, for example, the explanation of the term "capital" concludes with:

> These instructions were identical with those employed at the
> census of 1914 and 1909. The data compiled in respect to capital,
> however, at both censuses, as well as at all preceding censuses
> of manufactures, have been considered as being of limited value
> except as indicating very general conditions. While there are some
> establishments whose accounting systems are such that an ac-
> curate return for capital could be made, this is not true of the
> great majority, and the figures therefore do not show the actual
> amount of capital invested in different industries or in different
> localities (*Fourteenth Census,* Manufactures 1923, 11).

More important, it was not until the 1919 census that firms
were likely to have reported capital net of depreciation, based
on research by D. Creamer, D. Dobrovolsky, and I. Borenstein
(1960). They believe that a larger proportion of the capital figures were net of depreciation over time, as more firms adopted
the practice of accounting for depreciation. So the reported capital
values were likely to have overestimated the value of the capital stock, particularly in the beginning of the period under study.

The estimates in Table 3.5 are understood to be rough ap-
proximations, because of the inconsistency in the census definition of capital and our ignorance about how the firms measured capital. It is likely that the estimates of the northern returns
to capital in the earlier part of this period are understated relatively more than in the southern estimates, when gross capital
was the preferred definition of capital stock for the census reports. The northern textile capital stock was probably older than
the southern in a given census year, since there was no significant textile industry in the South prior to 1880. If gross capital
were adjusted for depreciation, there would be a larger percentage reduction in northern capital stock than in southern,
leading to a relatively greater upward adjustment in returns to
capital in the North.

In spite of the problems involved in measuring regional rates
of return, the finding that northern mills did not begin to experience a progressive decline in the industry until the 1920s is

relevant to understanding the pace of the textile industry relocation. Nationwide the textile industry fell into a depression after World War I. While corporate profits in general were booming in the 1920s, cotton manufacturing profits collapsed after 1919. Jules Backman and M. R. Gainsbrugh report that textile net income after taxes collectively fell from over $200 million in 1919 to about $100 million annually between 1920 and 1923, then turned to sizable losses in the mid–1920s (1946, 210).

The root of the textile depression was excess capacity. World War I stimulated the demand for cotton textiles required for the war effort, and mills either built additional capacity or operated multiple shifts to boost production. Night-shift operations became more prevalent, especially in the South. By expanding the hours of plant operation a mill owner could produce more without investing in additional equipment, which increased production capacity without changing the physical plant size. Economic models of shiftwork show that a firm is more likely to operate a second shift the higher capital's share of the firm's total costs (Betancourt and Clague 1981). Of course, the mill owner expands capacity at a cost in the sense that the equipment wears out faster, so in the long run machinery would have to be replaced sooner than if the mill were run on a single-shift basis.[4]

The response to wartime demand by the mills led to overcapacity in the textile industry when demand slowed in the postwar period. Mills continued to operate double shifts, which kept textile output growth strong and led to a decline in the price of cotton goods. Northern mills were hit harder than southern producers during this period because northern profit margins were thought to have been narrower than in the South. Although the South enjoyed a number of advantages well before the 1920s, including lower wages, "the decline in profit margins following 1920 laid bare the fundamental difference that existed between Northern and Southern operating costs" (Navin 1950, 340). The fact that the textile industry was competitive, in the sense that firms could not influence product prices, meant that northern mills could not stabilize prices to protect their profit margins.[5]

One southern advantage that emerged after the war was the use of night-shift operations, which was more common in the South than in the North. Multiple shifts allowed southern mills to lower their average costs of production in the near term, since fixed costs were spread over a higher volume of output in each period by operating the machinery and plant more intensively. Northern mills were restricted in running multiple shifts by local labor laws, which prevented the employment of women at night. Northern mills were forced to pay relatively high-wage male workers to run a second shift, so night shifts were limited in the North. Southern mills, on the other hand, could hire lower-wage female and child labor to work night shifts, which made multiple shifts more economical than in the North.

Explanations for the emergence of night work in the South vary, however. Navin argues that night shifts became socially acceptable during wartime, and this change in attitude persisted after the war (1950, 339). Wright (1981) points to disequilibrium in the labor market and the consequently high real wages in the 1920s as the reason southern mills employed labor in multiple shifts. Rising real wages also explain the northern collapse in that decade, he believes.

Although the pressures causing the rise in real textile wages in this period are examined at greater length in Chapter 8, a brief explanation of Wright's labor market argument helps to understand his hypothesis about southern night work. Wright suggests that real textile wages remained high after the wartime boost to real wages, because southern mill labor resisted nominal wage cuts that were required to reduce real wages in this period of price stability. In spite of excess supply in the labor markets in the South, according to various accounts, high real wages persisted. In some instances, nominal wage cuts were met with major strikes, which Wright asserts prevented employers from reducing wages sufficiently to lower real wages. Moreover, the failure of real farm wages to rise during the 1920s suggests that increases in real textile wages do not reflect higher opportunity costs, as measured by farm wages.

In a subsequent paper Martha Shiells and Wright (1983) show that a disequilibrium in real wages could induce mills to expand night work in a model where night labor is paid a premium and nominal wages do not adjust to an equilibrium level. In addition, they assume that mill management places night workers in jobs that raise labor productivity relative to the assignment that same worker would get in a daytime shift. In their model, real wages that are higher than the equilibrium level would cause a decrease in the employment of daytime labor, and a portion of those workers would seek night–shift work. Employers will hire more night labor, in spite of a rise in the basic wage rate, because the night-shift premium would decline to reduce the total compensation paid night labor. Some former day workers are nevertheless attracted to the night shift, because it may be preferred to unemployment. Firms might increase total output, in spite of an overall decline in total employment, if former daytime workers are placed in jobs that raise their productivity sufficiently to offset lost output due to lower overall employment.

Neither of these explanations for the development of excess capacity (night shifts) in the industry is satisfactory, however. Night work apparently was socially acceptable well before World War I, judging by the prevalence of shiftwork in prior years, especially in the South. For example, a 1907 survey by the Bureau of Labor Statistics found that over half of all mills in North Carolina operated with night shifts, and many other southern mills had formerly had a night shift (Wright 1981, 628).

Wright's argument that night work expanded in response to disequilibrium in the labor market is based on a number of assumptions that are difficult to support. Evidence of labor strikes and flat real farm wages is not sufficient to establish that textile wages were stuck above a market-clearing level in the 1920s. Labor strikes were not necessarily effective, and increases in mill-labor productivity could account for the divergence between mill and farm wages. Moreover, Shiells and Wright's model is based on a number of strong assumptions that are difficult to substantiate.[6] Traditional models of shiftwork are more appropriate to the case of the textile industry. Thus night work is probably best explained by attempts by mills to minimize costs by spreading fixed costs over a greater volume of production.

MILL DIRECTORIES

The comprehensive descriptions of textile mills found in the Davison's Textile Blue Book and the Official American Textile Directory provide more details about textile production in each region than can be found in the aggregated census reports. Directories for every five years beginning in 1885 and continuing through 1930 were used to furnish information on all operating mills producing cotton yarn or cloth in Massachusetts and North Carolina. These states will represent textile manufacturing in the North and South.

A summary of the data collected is provided in Table 3.6, which reports the average value among the mills that year for each characteristic described by the directories, followed by the number of mills that were included in that calculation in parentheses. Due to missing values in occasional incomplete mill entries in the directories, not all mills for a particular year were included in each calculation of the averages. The mill characteristics reported in the directories are listed at the left in the table. Capital is a current dollar value and is probably a rough approximation of the actual current value of mill capital, because it may not have been adjusted for depreciation.[7] Total spindles and looms are the mill equipment that is reported, along with details about ring and mule spindles. Population measures the size of the city in which the mill was located. The composition of mill spindles is indicated by the ratio of ring spindles to total spindles.

The last four rows in the table are percentages that indicate the share of total mills in the given year that have the "dummy" characteristic on the left, which measure the presence of steam power before 1905 and electric power thereafter, fine output, specialization in spinning, and survival to 1930. A dummy variable has a value of one if a characteristic is present and zero if not. A zero was assigned to the dummy variable in cases where there was no information on power, output, or number of looms. Electric power was not used until after 1900, so this dummy variable is not relevant until 1905. The survival dummy variable was based on whether a mill name appeared in the 1930 directory.

The summary statistics will be used to (1) compare the average mill in each state in each year, and (2) examine how the average mill changed from 1885 to 1930 in each region to compare the development pattern between the two regions.

Certain differences between the two regions were maintained throughout the period. The average northern mill was larger in terms of current dollar capital value, number of employees, and number of spindles and looms. The average population of a mill town was larger in the North. A larger share of northern mills produced fine output, which one would expect based on the census data that described regional output. A larger share of southern mills produced only yarn. Except for 1885 at least half of the southern mills were specialized in spinning, whereas only 15 to 20 percent of northern mills produced only yarn. The number of mills specialized in weaving was very small—at most fifteen in North Carolina (in 1925) and eighteen in Massachusetts (in 1925)—so this type of specialization will not be addressed in this study. The average percentage of ring spindles out of total spindles was noticeably greater in the southern mills, which is consistent with the belief that the adoption of the technological change embodied in the ring spindle occurred much more quickly in the South.

The interregional rankings varied over time for the remaining three variables. The average capital-labor ratio was greater for the northern mills through 1919, but in the 1920s, the capital-labor ratio became greater in the South compared with the North after almost doubling from the beginning of the period in both regions. Electric power was at first adopted by a somewhat larger share of northern mills in 1905, but thereafter a much larger share of southern mills were using electricity than in the North. The prevalence of night-shift operations in the South probably explains the much greater use of electric light in that region than in the North, where labor laws restrained the use of night work.

The evidence on survival rates suggests that the superiority of the southern textile industry relative to the North did not become apparent until the latter part of the 1880 to 1930 period. The southern rate of mill survival did not become much higher than that of the northern mills until 1915. In 1885 the northern

Table 3.6
Mean Values of Mill Characteristics*

North Carolina	1885	1895	1900	1905	1910	1915	1919	1925	1930
Number of Mills	76	125	173	232	290	291	339	384	332
Capital (thou$)	79 (32)	106 (77)	118 (141)	153 (195)	176 (257)	200 (251)	226 (287)	452 (315)	536 (262)
Labor	--	155 (65)	198 (116)	237 (179)	227 (214)	246 (212)	265 (241)	281 (258)	327 (233)
Capital/Labor	--	745 (46)	740 (97)	707 (155)	859 (190)	930 (187)	1035 (207)	1933 (227)	1862 (194)
Spindles	3658 (72)	4869 (121)	6180 (172)	9296 (231)	11413 (290)	12798 (291)	14292 (338)	15426 (384)	18776 (332)
Ring	--	0 (7)	6088 (112)	9067 (219)	11258 (280)	12487 (284)	14381 (325)	15377 (376)	18837 (323)
Mule	--	0 (7)	188 (112)	269 (219)	300 (280)	195 (284)	109 (325)	30 (376)	67 (323)
Loom	55 (74)	100 (125)	140 (173)	211 (232)	201 (290)	227 (291)	208 (339)	228 (383)	258 (331)
Population	1966 (47)	2510 (108)	3783 (145)	3576 (221)	5357 (283)	5524 (285)	5762 (334)	6759 (380)	7108 (330)
Ring/Spindles	--	--	.990 (104)	.984 (207)	.983 (274)	.989 (279)	.993 (318)	.998 (361)	.994 (312)
Electric Power	.000	--	--	.043	.279	.388	.590	.755	.801
Fine Output	--	.040	.069	.155	.207	.189	.218	.315	.328
Yarn Only	.407	.512	.520	.500	.566	.581	.628	.602	.587
Survived to 1930	.158	.304	.382	.466	.510	.577	.625	.747	--

Massachusetts	1885	1895	1900	1905	1910	1915	1919	1925	1930
Number of Mills	176	164	157	138	149	152	166	160	108
Capital (thou$)	551 (113)	584 (127)	628 (125)	730 (119)	891 (128)	1037 (130)	1093 (141)	1535 (129)	1422 (77)
Labor	-	660 (118)	692 (122)	802 (114)	838 (123)	883 (125)	931 (132)	861 (129)	735 (87)
Capital/Labor	-	1017 (102)	893 (105)	925 (102)	1016 (108)	1055 (106)	1194 (115)	1741 (109)	1760 (65)
Spindles	30731 (168)	43915 (158)	50255 (153)	59028 (138)	67763 (147)	73161 (149)	70463 (160)	73524 (152)	73488 (102)
Ring	-	11642 (12)	34154 (103)	42322 (129)	54256 (139)	57477 (142)	59175 (155)	64090 (147)	61536 (100)
Mule	-	15417 (12)	16764 (103)	14926 (129)	12252 (139)	11695 (142)	10105 (155)	8473 (147)	6502 (100)
Loom	728 (169)	984 (160)	1135 (156)	1482 (138)	1564 (149)	1601 (150)	1471 (161)	1514 (154)	1411 (104)
Population	21600 (165)	36795 (145)	47508 (140)	56361 (137)	64360 (149)	73098 (152)	76080 (166)	93468 (160)	96234 (108)
Ring/Spindles	-	.455 (7)	.722 (97)	.771 (122)	.841 (132)	.848 (133)	.872 (142)	.909 (129)	.930 (90)
Electric Power	-	-	-	.072	.201	.270	.331	.494	.574
Fine Output	.136	.226	.318	.362	.450	.487	.458	.444	.491
Yarn Only	.193	.220	.210	.159	.188	.191	.217	.169	.148
Survived to 1930	.227	.299	.357	.449	.483	.526	.524	.575	--

Source: Compiled by the author from Davison's Textile Blue Book, Official American Textile Directory, for the years cited.
* Number of mills reporting each characteristic shown in parentheses.

survival rate was about 7 percentage points higher than in the South. From 1895 to 1910 the southern survival share was greater than the northern, but by less than 3 percentage points. The similarity in regional survival rates up to the 1920s is consistent with the growth in number of mills in both regions through 1919, shown in the top row of Table 3.6. The directory evidence that the northern industry thrived to 1920, indicated by growth in the number of Massachusetts mills and survival rates as high as those in the South, corroborates the census data (discussed earlier) that showed growth in northern output and capacity through 1920.

Next, the changes in the characteristics of the average southern and northern mill can be traced. The number of southern mills continued to grow until the total peaked in 1925 and then dropped off in 1930. Average southern mill size generally grew through 1930, in terms of capital, employees, spindles, and looms. The capital-labor ratio rose through 1925 and then dropped somewhat in 1930. The average population of a mill town gradually increased each year except 1910.

The share of ring spindles in the South was large from the first year that data on the spindle composition were available, in 1900. Ring spindles were at least 98 percent of total spindles each year in the South, and the average number of mules steadily dropped after 1910. The share of output classified as "fine" increased each year, except in 1915, and approached one-third by 1930. The majority of southern mills produced only yarn after 1895, with that share peaking in 1919. The share of mills that survived to 1930 increased every year and exceeded 50 percent by 1910. Among southern mills operating in 1930, 86 percent had existed in 1925 and 14 percent originated sometime between 1925 and 1930.

The number of northern mills remained fairly steady up to the 1920s; there was a slight drop in the number of mills from 1885 to 1905, a rise up to 1919, then declines in 1925 and 1930. Growth in the number of northern mills up to the 1920s is consistent with similar patterns found in census data on northern output and machinery, which showed the northern branch of the industry remained viable during the period of development of the southern textile industry. In addition to mill count, the average value of mill capital grew through 1925, although other indicators of size—labor, spindles, and looms—tended to peak before that. The capital-labor ratio continued to rise through 1930. The average population of the mill towns increased steadily over the period.

Adoption of the ring spindle proceeded over the entire period in the North, which is indicated by the doubling of the share of ring spindles between 1895 and 1900 and the steady rise thereafter. The average number of mule spindles dropped each year after 1900, as northern mills apparently proceeded to abandon the mule in favor of the ring spindle.

The share of northern mills producing fine output increased steadily until 1915 and then varied between 44 to 49 percent thereafter. Most northern mills were integrated, doing both spinning and weaving; no more than 22 percent of the mills produced only yarn in any given year. The survival rate of the northern mills gradually rose throughout the period and became greater than 50 percent by 1915. In 1930 about 85 percent of the mills had been operating in 1925 and 15 percent were new, which is similar to the shares of existing and new mills in the South in 1930.

The profiles of the average mill in each region reveal that northern mills continued to expand, both in number and size, up to the 1920s, while the southern branch of the industry was developing at a rapid pace. The sharp decline of the northern textile industry in the 1920s, which has been documented by both aggregate census data and now by the data from the textile directories, will be explored in the following analysis of the factors contributing to mill survival and failure in that period.

NOTES

1. Total spindle capacity is directly related to the volume of production, except in cases where a mill operates multiple shifts or does not fully utilize capacity (some spindles are inactive).

2. Count indicates the yarn grade and is the measure of the number of 850 yard hanks in a pound of yarn.

3. Specifically, expenses included cost of material and power, wages and salaries, and miscellaneous expenses, which included rent, taxes,

repairs, insurance, and interest paid. Depreciation expense is not included, however, which prevents the calculation of accounting profits using the census data. Thus we refer to estimated net earnings and realize the limitations of these data. Galenson notes that without depreciation expense, the census data can only indicate "the ability of the industry in the two regions to earn profits" (1975, 204).

4. The rate of depreciation may depend more upon the rate of technological obsolescence than on the rate of utilization (wear and tear), however (Betancourt and Clague 1981, 18–32).

5. The total number of mills in the industry ranged from 905 in 1889 to a peak of 1,603 in 1922. The barriers to entry were considered quite low, and products were not branded, because mills usually sold fabrics in the gray (not colored) and in bulk. As a result prices were flexible and profits were low in the industry (Backman and Gainsbrugh 1946, 124, 142, 168).

6. In addition to "sticky" real wages, they assume that employers decrease the night-work premium when the base wage rises and that employers place former day workers in night-shift jobs that raise labor productivity relative to their daytime jobs (Shiells and Wright 1983).

7. An estimate of real mill capital, using 1880 as a base year, would raise the reported capital in 1885, 1895, and 1900, to account for deflation in the late nineteenth century. Thereafter the real capital values would be less than the current capital values, to adjust for inflation, which was particularly high in the World War I period.

4

Spindle Choice

REGIONAL DIFFERENCES IN SPINDLE CHOICE

The ring spindles became the more popular spindle choice in the textile industry in both regions in this period, but the switch to the ring spindle occurred much sooner in the South.[1] As noted in Chapter 2, ring spindles made up a larger share of textile spindles in the South than in the North, based on census data between 1890 and 1914 (see Table 2.1). The share of ring spindles was high from the start of the industry in the South, and by 1914 southern mills used the ring spindle almost exclusively. Northern mills also relied on the ring spindle to a greater extent over time, and the northern ring share rose to over 80 percent by 1914.

The choice of spindle depended on several factors: the fineness of yarn produced, input prices, whether the mill had mule spindles in place, and whether the mill was specialized in yarn production.[2] Regional differences in each of these variables contributed to the slower diffusion of the ring in the North.[3] The following discussion will elaborate on the relation between each of these factors and the choice between the mule and ring spindle. Then the importance of these parameters to the spindle decision will be examined based on the mill directory evidence.

When the ring spindle was first introduced it was confined

to use in spinning coarse yarn, because of the more frequent breakage of thread and less even twist than the mule (Galenson 1975, 77). The North could not switch completely to the ring spindle because northern mills produced the higher grades of yarn that could only be spun on the mule. But southern mills did not produce any fine yarns in 1890 and produced only 1 percent of U.S. fine–yarn output in 1900 (see Table 4.1), so the ring spindle could be used to a much greater extent than in the North.

The wage differential between skilled and unskilled mill workers was greater in the skilled-labor-scarce South than in the North (Galenson 1975, 80). This probably created a bigger cost advantage for the ring spindle over the mule for the southern mills than the northern mills, for a given grade of yarn. Lars Sandberg (1969) argues that since the ring used unskilled labor and the mule required the relatively high-wage mule spinner, the ring had a cost advantage in spinning lower count yarn that stemmed from a lower labor cost. Rings were more labor intensive than mules at low counts, but the relative factor intensities reversed at finer grades.[4] The labor cost advantage from choosing the ring for coarser yarns would be more pronounced for the southern mills.

The northern mills may have rationally waited longer than the southern mills to switch to the ring spindle because of dif-

Table 4.1
Southern Cotton Yarn Production
(as Share of U.S. Total)

Year	Coarse	Medium	Fine	Total
1889	.411	.032	.000	.233
1899	.525	.259	.011	.400
1909	.624	.417	.236	.506
1919	.708	.483	.269	.576

Source: Census of Manufactures

ferences in the quantity and age of mule spindles installed in each region when the new technology was introduced. The northern mill, typically established pre-1880, would continue using its mule spindles if the variable costs of spinning with the mules were less than the total costs of purchasing and operating the rings.

Southern mills would have faced a different choice. The southern mills considering a spindle purchase were more likely to be new, with no spindles installed, or to have equipment that had been bought used from the North. Uttley reports that "the earliest Southern mills were not in all cases up-to-date concerns, some of them being equipped with discarded machinery from the North" (1905, 44). Mitchell concurs that "just at first some second-hand equipment was installed, less from desire of New England mills to put this off on their new rivals, than from innocence and necessity of Southern beginners" (1921, 245). Since some of the used spindles would be near the end of their useful lifetimes, the southern mills may have been more likely to scrap any mules installed than the northern mills using mules. Hence the southern mills would essentially have been thinking of equipping the entire mill. They would have considered the total costs of operating with each type of spindle, since the cost of the mule equipment was not a sunk cost, as it was for the northern mill with operative mules installed.

Studies of the adoption of the automatic loom suggest the impact of the type and vintage of equipment already in place on the rate of adoption of new technology. Irwin Feller (1966) found in his study of the diffusion of the Draper loom that northern mills rationally delayed switching to the new model when it was first introduced. Feller's calculations show that the new loom technology had a cost advantage before 1910 in the North if a mill was choosing between the standard and the automatic loom, but not if the standard loom was already installed.

Feller shows that it was possible for the higher capital costs of the automatic Draper loom to absorb the lower labor costs that could be achieved, to the point that the variable costs of the plain loom were lower than the total costs of the Draper loom. Based on 1903 statistics, for example, the wage bill with installed plain looms was on average .3 percent lower than the total costs of production with Draper looms (Feller 1966, 341). By 1910, however, the margin of cost savings with installed plain looms had narrowed to the point that their advantage over Draper looms was no longer clear. The automatic loom's position relative to plain looms improved over time because of a general decline in interest rates and rise in wages which favored the Draper loom.

Although the cost estimates for spinning with the two types of spindle are not available, the logic of Feller's approach leads to the suggestion that the ring spindle, like the Draper loom, may have been adopted less completely in the north because of the profitability of continuing to operate the stock of mules in place. Installed mule spindles may have had an advantage relative to new ring spindles if capital costs swamped the labor-cost savings of the ring spindles. Total costs with ring spindles could have been lower than the variable costs of operating mule spindles at sufficiently low interest rates and high wage rates, however, which could have led to an improvement in the relative savings with the ring spindle in the North.

Vertical specialization also may have played a role in spindle choice, by hindering diffusion of the ring spindle. William Lazonick (1981) claims vertical specialization in either spinning or weaving was a constraint preventing the introduction of ring spinning in specialized British spinning mills prior to World War I. Specialization required that finished yarn had to be shipped to the weaving mills, which added transportation costs to the spinning production costs. The ring-spun yarn was more costly to ship because it was wound on heavy wooden bobbins, whereas mule-spun yarn was wound into packages on the bare spindle. Investment in the ring by specialized spinning mills was also discouraged by the greater uncertainty about the demand for ring-spun yarn by the weaver and supplies of ring-spun yarn from the spinner if these functions were not coordinated, as they would be within a vertically integrated mill (1981, 106). Lazonick's work is applicable to the U.S. mills as well. Copeland (1912) notes that the ring spindles used in the U.S. also required heavy bobbins, thus creating additional transportation costs that an integrated mill could avoid by spinning yarn for its own use. But this disadvantage may have been alleviated by the introduction of ring spinning machines equipped with paper tubes after 1900 (Saxonhouse and Wright 1983, 21).

Gary Saxonhouse and Wright (1983) are skeptical about the importance of vertical specialization in the choice of spindle technique, however, based on their investigation of worldwide use of the two types of spindles. Two counter-examples suggest that factors other than the degree of specialization guided spindle choice in each country.[5] Japan switched to rings in the late nineteenth century, when mills were still specialized. In Russia spinning was dominated by integrated mills, yet orders for new mule spindles continued to be placed well into the twentieth century.

Saxonhouse and Wright also question whether vertical specialization and the cost of transporting wooden ring bobbins was a constraint on the adoption of the ring spindle. In light of the development of paper tubes, mentioned earlier, the potential constraint imposed by specialization could have been alleviated by switching to the new tubes. The English industry did not adopt the paper tubes, however, in spite of the structure of the British industry. They argue that British spinners would have utilized paper tubes if vertical specialization was the factor that hindered their adoption of the ring spindle (Saxonhouse and Wright 1983, 23).

DIRECTORY EVIDENCE ON SPINDLE CHOICE

The average share of ring spindles as a proportion of total spindles among mills in each representative state was calculated from the descriptions of mill equipment in the textile directories, as shown in Table 4.2. The southern mills appear to have relied almost exclusively on the ring spindle as early as 1900. The average ring share in the South was near 100 percent, which is consistent with earlier evidence that documented the average number of ring and mule spindles per mill. In the North the average ring share rose steadily, from 72 percent in 1900 to 93 percent by 1930.

The average ring share remained significantly higher in the

Table 4.2
Regional Differences in Ratio of Ring Spindles to Total Spindles

North Carolina	Year	Ring Share	Std.Dev.	No. Mills
	1900	.990	.098	104
	1905	.984	.120	207
	1910	.983	.122	274
	1915	.989	.097	279
	1919	.993	.070	318
	1925	.998	.035	361
	1930	.994	.066	312
Massachusetts	Year	Ring Share	Std.Dev.	No. Mills
	1900	.722	.270	97
	1905	.771	.240	122
	1910	.841	.204	132
	1915	.848	.209	133
	1919	.872	.189	142
	1925	.909	.166	129
	1930	.930	.152	90

Year	Difference in Shares	Test Statistic*
1900	.268	9.24
1905	.213	9.18
1910	.142	7.40
1915	.141	7.42
1919	.121	7.42
1925	.089	6.05
1930	.064	3.89

* The hypothesis of no difference in shares was rejected at the .001 confidence level in all cases.

South than in the North throughout the period, confirming that the new spindle technology was diffused more completely among the southern mills than in the North. A test of the hypothesis that the average ring share was different between the regions yields test statistics that are significant at the 1 percent level each year (see Table 4.2).

Some of the determinants of spindle choice discussed earlier can be evaluated with this data set. The effect of the type of output produced, fine or other, and mill structure, specialized or integrated, can be analyzed directly by comparing the use of ring spindles by mills categorized by output and structure. Without data on equipment inventories detailing the age distribution of a mill's spindles, the effect of installed spindles on spindle choice can only be studied indirectly by using mill age as a proxy for the average age of installed equipment. Lacking data on mill costs, the effect of factor prices on spindle choice cannot be specified, however.

The use of mule spindles was clearly associated with the production of fine output in the North (see Table 4.3). Mills with fine output reported far higher average mules per mill and lower ring shares than producers of lower grades of output. Surprisingly, in the South the case is reversed—fine output producers have higher ring shares and fewer average mules per mill. It is probably correct to generalize that all southern mills, regardless of output grade, relied heavily on the ring spindle. The constraint imposed by the type of output a mill produced may have been relevant only before the turn of the century, due to improvements in the spindle design that eventually made the ring suitable for spinning all grades of yarn. Since the South did not begin to produce fine output until the refinements in the ring were made, the association of fine grades with ring use can be reconciled with the relationship between fine output and mule spindles found among the northern mills.

The hypothesized association between the vertical integration of spinning and weaving and a preference for the ring spindle finds support in the southern data, but only in the year 1900 for the northern data (see Table 4.4). Southern mills that were specialized in spinning (a majority of the North Carolina mills) had more mule spindles per mill and somewhat lower ring shares each year compared to the integrated mills. The ring shares were very high for both types of mills, however. In the North specialized mills were in the minority. With the exception of 1900, the specialized mills had higher average levels of mules per mill and ring shares than the integrated mills. Perhaps mill structure was less relevant to the northern mill's choice of spindle than some other determinants. Another pos-

Table 4.3
Spindle Choice in Mills Classified by Grade of Output

		Fine Output		Other Output	
	Year	Mules	Ring/Spindles	Mules	Ring/Spindles
North Carolina					
	1895	--	--	0	--
		--	--	(7)	--
	1900	0	1.000	206	.989
		(10)	(9)	(102)	(95)
	1905	111	.994	301	.983
		(36)	(35)	(183)	(172)
	1910	0	1.000	379	.979
		(58)	(56)	(222)	(218)
	1915	0	1.000	241	.987
		(54)	(52)	(230)	(227)
	1919	0	1.000	138	.991
		(69)	(68)	(256)	(250)
	1925	0	1.000	43	.997
		(117)	(111)	(259)	(250)
	1930	97	.989	51	.996
		(107)	(106)	(216)	(206)
Massachusetts					
	1895	0	1.000	26429	.353
		(5)	(1)	(7)	(6)
	1900	39444	.630	12632	.760
		(30)	(28)	(73)	(69)
	1905	22286	.710	10564	.810
		(48)	(47)	(81)	(75)
	1910	19844	.774	6139	.900
		(62)	(62)	(77)	(70)
	1915	18554	.798	5026	.901
		(70)	(69)	(72)	(64)
	1919	17771	.815	3626	.928
		(71)	(71)	(84)	(71)
	1925	15061	.853	3104	.967
		(66)	(65)	(81)	(64)
	1930	11114	.885	1702	.989
		(51)	(51)	(49)	(39)

Note: Number of mills reporting each characteristic shown in parentheses.

sibility is that the switch to the ring may have been inhibited in integrated mills by the concomitant slowness to adopt the automatic loom in the North.

The mills were separated into categories by a proxy for mill age to examine the effect of the replacement decision on the choice of spindle. Creating mill age categories separates mills into groups likely to have compared the total costs of each spindle type, the newest and oldest mills, and those likely to have compared the variable costs of installed and operating spindles to the total costs of purchased spindles. Each year mills in the two regions were categorized by an estimate of how long the mills had been in operation, based on all the previous years' mill data from the directories, from 1885 to the year under consideration. Since some mills were in operation before 1885, the lifetimes for these mills will be underestimated (primarily northern mills). As a result, the highest age category is understood to include all mills that age and older. One deficiency of this approach is that a mill's age does not necessarily correspond to the age of its equipment, since a mill was likely to be continually replacing worn equipment. The mean values for the mill characteristics, categorized by age, are shown for 1910 and 1925 in Table 4.5.

The age distribution of mills was very different in each region, as would be expected when comparing one region where an industry had been long-established with a region where the industry was recently introduced. In the North the highest mill frequency occurred in the oldest mill category each year. Throughout the period roughly half of the mills in operation had existed since 1885 or before. In the South, in contrast, the new mills had the greatest frequency each year, with the smallest frequency in the oldest age category. Roughly a third of the southern mills were new each year.

In both regions the newest and the oldest mills had higher ring-spindle ratios compared to the middle-aged mills. In fact, new mills opening in 1925 used rings exclusively in both regions. The oldest mills in the North appeared to be replacing their mule spindles, as well as adding to their total spindle stock, with ring spindles from 1910 to 1925. The oldest southern mills were already using only ring spindles by 1910. These results fit the hypothesis that mills in the extreme age groups were more likely to choose the ring spindle than mills in the middle age groups. New mills had no installed spindles and the oldest mills were ready to scrap their installed spindles. These mills would

Table 4.4
Comparison of Specialized and Integrated Mills*

North Carolina	Spinning Mills				Integrated			
	1900	1910	1919	1930	1900	1910	1919	1930
Number of Mills	90	164	213	195	83	126	126	137
Capital (thou$)	89 (76)	118 (147)	174 (187)	428 (156)	152 (65)	253 (110)	322 (100)	695 (106)
Labor	118 (57)	150 (115)	172 (144)	215 (134)	275 (59)	317 (99)	404 (97)	479 (99)
Capital/Labor	853 (49)	934 (102)	1094 (127)	1912 (112)	626 (48)	772 (88)	942 (80)	1795 (82)
Spindles	5061 (90)	8239 (164)	10688 (212)	14744 (195)	7408 (82)	15545 (126)	20356 (126)	24515 (137)
Ring	4672 (59)	7805 (154)	10722 (203)	14674 (186)	7665 (53)	15480 (126)	20469 (122)	24489 (137)
Mule	356 (59)	492 (154)	129 (203)	96 (186)	0 (53)	66 (126)	75 (122)	26 (137)
Loom	0 (90)	0 (164)	0 (213)	0 (195)	291 (83)	463 (126)	559 (126)	629 (136)
Population	3095 (75)	3893 (158)	4671 (208)	6237 (193)	4520 (70)	7208 (125)	7563 (126)	8334 (137)
Ring/Spindles	.983 (59)	.976 (154)	.992 (203)	.991 (186)	1.000 (45)	.992 (120)	.996 (115)	.999 (126)
Electric Power	–	.268	.573	.785	.096	.294	.619	.825
Fine Output	.044	.220	.268	.431	.096	.190	.135	.182
Survived to 1930	.400	.500	.615	–	.361	.524	.643	–

56

Massachusetts	Spinning Mills				Integrated			
	1900	1910	1919	1930	1900	1910	1919	1930
Number of Mills	33	28	36	16	124	124	131	92
Capital (thou$)	554	894	853	930	645	890	1158	1521
	(23)	(21)	(30)	(13)	(102)	(107)	(111)	(64)
Labor	318	378	500	435	779	917	1028	782
	(23)	(18)	(24)	(12)	(99)	(105)	(108)	(75)
Capital/Labor	1205	1067	1248	1719	829	1007	1182	1769
	(18)	(15)	(21)	(11)	(87)	(93)	(94)	(54)
Spindles	33571	38697	49813	44646	54843	74601	76036	78077
	(33)	(28)	(34)	(14)	(120)	(119)	(126)	(88)
Ring	17355	32323	46070	44646	37712	59066	62720	64285
	(18)	(25)	(33)	(14)	(85)	(114)	(122)	(86)
Mule	19425	3818	4598	0	16200	14102	11595	7561
	(18)	(25)	(33)	(14)	(85)	(114)	(122)	(86)
Loom	0	0	0	0	1440	1925	1894	1668
	(33)	(28)	(36)	(16)	(123)	(121)	(125)	(88)
Population	32351	43149	59750	74656	51297	69269	80602	99986
	(28)	(28)	(36)	(16)	(112)	(121)	(130)	(92)
Ring/Spindles	.664	.891	.921	1.000	.735	.829	.857	.917
	(18)	(25)	(33)	(14)	(79)	(107)	(109)	(76)
Electric Power	–	.214	.222	.625	–	.194	.359	.565
Fine Output	.303	.464	.444	.563	.323	.435	.458	.478
Survived to 1930	.242	.429	.417	–	.387	.492	.550	–

Source: Compiled by the author from Davison's Textile Blue Book, Official American Textile Directories, for the years cited.
* Number of mills reporting each characteristic shown in parentheses.

Table 4.5
Age Composition of Mills: 1910 and 1925*

North Carolina – 1910	Years Old				
	0	5	10	15	25
Number of Mills	100	72	45	44	29
Capital (thou$)	167	186	173	156	213
	(87)	(63)	(43)	(38)	(26)
Labor	151	244	267	236	267
	(52)	(59)	(42)	(36)	(25)
Capital/Labor	1111	881	765	633	759
	(44)	(52)	(41)	(31)	(22)
Spindles	9409	12284	15044	11915	9793
	(100)	(72)	(45)	(44)	(29)
Ring	9535	12003	14614	11604	9793
	(96)	(70)	(42)	(43)	(29)
Mule	55	459	753	349	0
	(96)	(70)	(42)	(43)	(29)
Loom	143	168	246	284	287
	(100)	(72)	(45)	(44)	(29)
Population	5128	6478	4605	6432	2996
	(99)	(70)	(43)	(42)	(29)
Ring/Spindles	.998	.964	.976	.976	1.000
	(91)	(70)	(42)	(42)	(29)
Electric Power	.440	.208	.133	.318	.069
Fine Output	.250	.194	.156	.205	.172
Yarn Only	.620	.667	.556	.432	.345
Survived to 1930	.400	.583	.600	.614	.414

58

Massachusetts -- 1910	Years Old				
	0	5	6	15	25
Number of Mills	21	16	6	21	88
Capital (thou$)	765	816	900	709	975
	(19)	(13)	(5)	(18)	(73)
Labor	387	515	1170	833	938
	(11)	(13)	(5)	(18)	(76)
Capital/Labor	1367	1280	1078	898	944
	(10)	(11)	(4)	(16)	(67)
Spindles	44928	50760	100145	82925	70827
	(20)	(16)	(5)	(20)	(86)
Ring	36521	35320	58936	65744	58641
	(20)	(13)	(4)	(19)	(83)
Mule	8407	11615	16245	15440	12356
	(20)	(13)	(4)	(19)	(83)
Loom	557	976	2126	1922	1796
	(21)	(16)	(6)	(20)	(86)
Population	78753	96812	85204	53132	55965
	(21)	(16)	(6)	(20)	(86)
Ring/Spindles	.816	.770	.788	.853	.855
	(17)	(10)	(4)	(19)	(82)
Electric Power	.286	.438	.167	.095	.159
Fine Output	.524	.625	.667	.524	.352
Yarn Only	.476	.250	.000	.381	.068
Survived to 1930	.524	.375	1.000	.476	.455

Table 4.5 (continued)

North Carolina - 1925	\	\	\	Years Old	\	\	\	\
	0	5	10	15	20	25	30	40
Number of Mills	109	57	25	56	52	34	33	18
Capital (thou$)	472	332	428	369	555	626	465	359
	(84)	(46)	(20)	(48)	(41)	(31)	(27)	(18)
Labor	183	180	270	322	299	399	386	256
	(53)	(32)	(20)	(36)	(43)	(32)	(27)	(15)
Capital/Labor	2686	2009	2092	1708	1758	1859	1261	1435
	(46)	(27)	(17)	(32)	(36)	(30)	(24)	(15)
Spindles	10180	11626	18419	20029	18149	22893	18216	13652
	(109)	(57)	(25)	(56)	(52)	(34)	(33)	(18)
Ring	10139	11585	18419	20029	18179	21981	18216	13652
	(106)	(54)	(25)	(56)	(51)	(33)	(33)	(18)
Mule	0	0	0	0	221	0	0	0
	(106)	(54)	(25)	(56)	(51)	(33)	(33)	(18)
Loom	108	74	222	341	260	385	439	320
	(109)	(57)	(25)	(56)	(52)	(33)	(33)	(18)
Population	5432	7222	6398	7032	7953	5856	9583	6194
	(108)	(57)	(24)	(56)	(51)	(34)	(32)	(18)
Ring/Spindles	1	1	1	1	.987	1	1	1
	(93)	(53)	(25)	(56)	(51)	(33)	(32)	(18)
Electric Power	.798	.789	.800	.786	.731	.647	.848	.389
Fine Output	.376	.351	.120	.429	.327	.147	.242	.167
Yarn Only	.606	.737	.600	.661	.635	.529	.424	.333
Survived to 1930	.688	.772	.800	.714	.808	.794	.818	.667

Massachusetts - 1925

	Years Old							
	0	5	10	15	20	25	30	40
Number of Mills	17	12	11	14	14	6	16	70
Capital (thou$)	210	929	1271	1853	2476	2838	1000	1597
	(5)	(11)	(9)	(14)	(11)	(4)	(15)	(60)
Labor	335	852	470	697	1186	1331	461	1017
	(10)	(9)	(6)	(12)	(11)	(4)	(14)	(63)
Capital/Labor	1891	2532	1629	2046	1951	1902	1381	1606
	(3)	(8)	(5)	(12)	(9)	(3)	(13)	(56)
Spindles	15617	64477	59654	83329	83782	128724	60490	85133
	(15)	(12)	(10)	(14)	(13)	(5)	(16)	(67)
Ring	14376	64477	32522	72864	71834	89218	46828	77883
	(14)	(12)	(9)	(14)	(13)	(4)	(15)	(66)
Mule	0	0	11538	10465	11947	21687	17162	7510
	(14)	(12)	(9)	(14)	(13)	(4)	(15)	(66)
Loom	145	1017	985	984	1239	3400	1305	2063
	(16)	(12)	(10)	(14)	(13)	(5)	(15)	(69)
Population	92393	85656	156033	140055	128860	100943	63755	74991
	(17)	(12)	(11)	(14)	(14)	(6)	(16)	(70)
Ring/Spindles	1.000	1.000	.774	.878	.851	.873	.877	.934
	(7)	(6)	(8)	(13)	(11)	(4)	(15)	(65)
Electric Power	.706	.917	.455	.429	.500	.333	.313	.443
Fine Output	.176	.083	.636	.714	.500	.667	.563	.429
Yarn Only	.235	.333	.091	.500	.000	.000	.438	.057
Surviving to 1930	.294	.500	.727	.786	.429	1.000	.625	.571

Source: Compiled by the author from Davison's Textile Blue Book, Offical American Textile Directory, for the years cited.
* Number of mills reporting each characteristic shown in parentheses.

have compared the total costs of each type of spindle, a calculation that favored the ring spindle. The mills in the middle
categories had installed spindles that were likely to have remaining lifetimes, which was a condition that favored the continued use of the mule spindle.

REGIONAL FACTOR PRICE DIFFERENTIALS
AND SPINDLE CHOICE

Regional factor prices also played a role in the choice between the ring and the mule spindle, since the spindles had
different factor requirements. Production costs varied between
the two types of spindle for a given set of factor prices, because
resources were used in different combinations for each technique. Which type of spindle was chosen to minimize costs
would depend on factor prices in that region.

A model that illustrates the relationship between the choice
of spindle and factor prices is shown in Figure 4.1. Unit-value
isoquants represent the combinations of capital and labor required to produce one unit worth of product, in this case yarn.
The more expensive ring spindle had lower labor requirements

Figure 4.1
Model for Spindle Choice

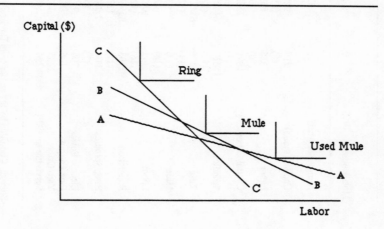

than the mule spindle for a unit value of output. The used mule spindle is assumed to require more labor input but a lower capital expenditure than a new mule spindle. More labor is required because older equipment is more likely to break down, which demands more labor time to produce the same amount of output. In addition, used equipment is likely to be less efficient, depending on its condition.

This analysis oversimplifies by treating labor as a homogeneous input and ignores for now the alleged differences in the quality of each regional labor force. The skilled-labor-saving aspect of the ring spindle is therefore not treated explicitly in this model. Also, this model does not consider the case of the mill that has spindles in place, with fixed capital costs treated as sunk costs for installed spindles. As noted earlier, a mill with existing mule spindles would have compared the variable costs of the installed mule spindles to the total costs of purchasing new ring spindles. This model, on the other hand, considers only the case where the total costs of operating each type of spindle are compared. Thus new mills, mills expanding capacity, and those replacing worn equipment best fit the circumstances that are relevant to this model.

The model isolates the effect of changes in regional factor prices on the choice of spindle in each region. Figure 4.1 illustrates the various spindle choices corresponding to factor price ratios in the beginning of the period and at the end of the period. The initial factor price ratio in the beginning of the period is not equal in the two regions. Historians recognize that the South was a capital-scarce region, where the ratio of wages to the rental rate of capital was lower than in the North. Interest rates in the South were higher than in the North, and southern wages were lower than northern.[6] By the end of the period, however, interest rates and wages tended to equalize between the two regions, so that the same wage-rental rate prevailed in both regions. In particular the textile wage differential between North Carolina and Massachusetts tended to diminish unevenly over the period 1880 to 1930, as we discuss in greater detail in Chapter 8.

The model predicts that the southern mills would choose to purchase used mule spindles when the wage-rental rate ratio was relatively low in the late nineteenth century. In fact the southern mills were known to have relied on used equipment from the North until the early twentieth century, as mentioned earlier. The southern mills would have been concerned with saving on capital costs in the early period when southern interest rates were high. In the latter part of the period, after wages had risen and interest rates declined, the southern mills would have been likely to choose the ring spindle, according to this model. The switch to the ring spindle is shown by the tangency of the higher wage-rental rate line with the ring spindle isoquant as the factor price line rises from A to C.

In the North the mule spindle was the appropriate choice in the beginning of the period when the wage-rental rate ratio was relatively low in that region, shown by line B. As wages rose during the period, the northern mills had an incentive to switch to the labor-saving ring spindle. The switch to the ring spindle is illustrated by the rise in the factor price line from B to C.

At the end of the period, after wages had risen in both regions and factor prices had tended to equalize between regions, the model predicts that the ring spindle would be favored for production in both regions. The evidence from the directories supports this analysis. The ring spindle gained popularity in both the North and South throughout the period, as indicated by a rise in the average share of ring spindles in total spindles in each region.

Since the model is applicable to mills that were choosing between purchasing either type of spindle, rather than mills with installed spindles, the behavior of new mills is a better test of the validity of the model. When mills were grouped according to age in the earlier discussion of the directory evidence, it was discovered that new mills in either region revealed a stronger preference for the ring spindle in the latter part of this period compared to the mills in earlier directories. That result is consistent with the prediction based on the model, in which rising wages and declining capital rental rates would lead to a preference for the ring spindle.

NOTES

1. In his study of the Draper loom, Feller (1966) clarifies that the North lagged behind the South in the adoption of new loom technology if the automatic loom as a share of total looms is compared, but that in absolute terms, the cumulative number of automatic looms sold to the northern mills exceeded sales to the South in the period 1894–1914.

2. Fineness is measured by yarn count. Counts 0–20 are coarse, 20–40 are medium, and above 40 are fine.

3. This explanation for spindle choice is based on the neoclassical model for a firm that makes profit-maximizing choices given the existing constraints, including available techniques and exogenous factor prices. Lazonick (1981) presents an alternative theoretical framework for the study of the diffusion of the ring and automatic loom that considers the institutional constraints the firm faces, including labor relations and the industrial structure of the regional textile industry.

4. Sandberg (1969) argues that rings were the rational choice up to a count of forty for British mills in the early–twentieth century.

5. Saxonhouse and Wright (1983, 16–19) suggest that the quality of local cotton may have determined a nation's choice of spindle. The ring spindle required a long–fiber cotton, but the mule spindle could be used with a short-staple cotton. Nations using the ring spindle, the United States and Brazil, grew the higher quality, long-staple type of cotton. Mules were preferred in India, where short-staple cotton was grown, and in Britain and Russia, where short-staple cotton was imported. Differences in the type of spindle used within countries seem to dispute their argument, however. Availability of a particular quality of cotton will not be a factor in explaining regional differences in spindle choice in the United States.

6. Galenson (1975) notes that southern interest rates may not measure the southern mill cost of borrowing, since a system of financial intermediation was not developed in the South in this period. Southern borrowing costs were still higher than in the North, however, since the northern machine companies and other lenders charged a premium on funds for the southern mills (see Chapter 2).

5

Mill Survival

METHODOLOGY

The mill directory evidence provides an opportunity to trace the progress and decline of individual cotton textile mills as the relocation of the U.S. textile industry gradually proceeded up to 1930. The distinguishing characteristics of the mills that survived in each region help identify the strategies that led to the expansion of the industry in both the North and the South through the 1920s. Here, the study of changes in the textile industry in each region, discussed in Chapter 3, is expanded on by isolating those trends that fueled the growth of the regional industries.

The study of the textile mills that survived to 1930 progressed in two stages. This chapter reports the first step: describing the two types of mills, surviving and nonsurviving, based on the statistics derived from the mill directories. Profiles of surviving and nonsurviving mills in each region at different times are compared to find distinguishing characteristics that might have led to either survival or failure. The next step builds on the preliminary findings by testing the relationships between mill survival and various mill characteristics that are thought to be important in determining survival. Statistical regression analysis of both the probability of mill survival and growth in mill capacity, measured by total spindles, is discussed in Chapter 6.

This approach to the study of firm survival is loosely based on the "survivor technique" that was developed by George Stigler. Stigler (1968) devised a method for determining the optimum firm size, or range of sizes, in an industry based on the outcome of competition among firms of different sizes in that industry. The size of firms that performed better than other firms in an industry would indicate the optimum scale of operation in that industry. Rather than measure the actual costs of firms of different sizes, or calculate the hypothetical costs of different sizes of plants, Stigler suggests that optimum firm size can be determined by observing that "the competition of different sizes of firms sifts out the more efficient enterprises" (1968, 73).

The survivor technique to find optimum firm size classifies firms into various size categories and calculates the share of industry output attributed to each category over time. Classes in which market share falls over time are considered inefficient firm sizes, and efficient firm sizes are revealed by those classes in which market share rises. In cases where sales or production are not reported by individual companies, firm size and market share can be measured by capacity.

Although the present study is not designed to find the optimum firm size in the textile industry, certain aspects of the survivor technique are applicable to research of growth in the industry in each region. First, firm efficiency is deduced by survival in the industry, rather than by measurement of each firm's costs and profits. In this case the historical records of firm costs, revenues, and profits are not available for most southern mills before 1930, so a regional comparison of efficiency in each region would not have been possible in any event. Second, growth in industry capacity can be taken as an indicator of firm survival when production data are not available. In this study growth in a mill's total spindle stock is measured as a proxy for expansion of mill capacity, following the example of other tests using the survivor technique. Analysis of growth in mill spindle stock is postponed until the next chapter.

This study of firm survival in the textile industry is based on a large sample of mills from representative states in the North and the South between 1885 and 1930. All of the cotton textile mills operating in Massachusetts and North Carolina during this period have been identified with the use of two textile directories, the Davison's Textile Blue Book and the Official American Textile Directory. A mill is considered to have survived to the end of the period if the mill name appears in the 1930 directory. A mill must be listed under the same name to be treated as a survivor, so where mergers or consolidations occurred and the mill name changed, the mill is treated as a nonsurvivor along with the failing mills.[1] In any given year prior to 1930, mills in the sample can be identified as either survivors or non-survivors, since a mill's record of entries in one of the above directories has been traced through 1930.

Based on the economic model of a competitive industry, survival in the cotton textile industry is assumed to depend upon whether a mill earns non-negative profits in the long run. Economic theory of competitive markets holds that a firm survives in the short run as long as the price for its product exceeds the average variable costs of production, and the firm continues to operate in the long run if profits are non-negative. A firm shuts down, or fails, if the product price does not cover average variable costs in the short run. For a competitive firm, profits in the textile industry were determined by textile yarn and cloth prices, mill wages, capital equipment prices, interest rates, and other costs of production. In economic models that allow for uncertainty, the quality of firm management is also recognized to be a determinant of profits.

Once mills are identified as either survivors or nonsurvivors, potential links between survival and the mill characteristics listed in the directories can be examined. The hypothesized association between survival and these production parameters is built on several underlying assumptions, however, which should be clarified. The various parameters that each mill reported in the directories are thought to reflect cost-minimizing, profit-maximizing management decisions. Those decisions were influenced by product and factor prices that the mills in each region faced. Actually, mill survival depended directly on mill profitability and those management choices about production parameters. But in the absence of evidence on local factor prices and individual mill profits, descriptions of the mills from the directories are assumed to reflect the factor price conditions of each region and to provide the observable link in the relationship between profit conditions and regional mill survival.

Implicit in the following discussion of mill characteristics and survival is the assumption that each mill characteristic was based on a cost-minimizing decision. The size of the mill, described by the capital value, number of employees, or number of machines, depends on capital costs (the rental rate, interest rate, and price of machinery), wages, and the presence of economies of scale.[2] Changes in mill size over time may also reflect profit expectations. The capital-labor ratio depends on the factor price ratio. The capital intensity will be lower, the lower the wage-rental rate ratio.

As discussed in Chapter 4, the ring-spindle ratio is probably determined by several variables, including factor costs, type of output, and age of the mill's stock of equipment. The wage-rental rate ratio had to be sufficiently high to induce a mill to adopt the more expensive, but labor-saving, ring spindle. Converting to electric power involved a comparison of the costs of the alternative power sources: electricity, steam (which required coal), and the water wheel. The choice of yarn or cloth type and the grade of output was probably constrained by the skills of the regional labor force in the South, but also depended on the expectations of the prices for the various textile products and a mill's willingness to risk the fluctuations in demand that were more common in the higher grade fabrics.

The Davison's Textile Blue Book has been used previously to study mill survival and failure, but only on a limited scale. T. R. Smith (1944) investigated the Fall River, Massachusetts, mills listed in the Davison's directory in 1925 to compare those that subsequently failed to the surviving mills. Of the total forty-four mills operating in Fall River in 1925, twenty-six later failed. Smith hypothesized that the type of goods produced was an important determinant of survival, and that print-cloth mills were especially susceptible to collapse in the 1920s. Analysis of the directory information about the types of output each mill produced supported Smith's theory. Among Fall River mills producing only print cloth, 90 percent failed, whereas 45 percent of the mills producing fine goods collapsed (1944, 128). Smith's work not only points to the value of the mill directories, but provides insight into the likely role played by the northern strategy to shift to fine grades of output as growth in the southern industry progressed. The following analysis expands the approach first taken by Smith to include the South and the rest of the North, a longer period of investigation, and a wider range of parameters in addition to the type of output produced by the mills to advance the study of the relocation of the industry.

DESCRIPTION OF SURVIVORS AT INDUSTRY LEVEL

On the national level the textile mills that survived in the U.S. textile industry in either region can be distinguished from the mills that failed on the basis of several characteristics. The surviving mills were larger than the nonsurvivors, as measured by capital value, employees, and number of spindles and looms. The capital-labor ratio was generally smaller for the surviving mills, with exceptions in 1900 and 1910. The advances in machinery and power were adopted sooner by the surviving mills, as measured by the share of ring spindles and the share of mills using electricity. A larger share of the surviving mills produced fine output, and a smaller proportion were specialized spinning mills, compared with the nonsurviving mills. The average population of cities in which the surviving mills were located was larger than for the nonsurvivors. The surviving mills had a lower average age than the nonsurviving mills in 1900, but thereafter the average age in each group was nearly equal. Table 5.1 shows the average values of these characteristics for the two groups of mills in selected years.

The comparison between the surviving and failing mills suggests that certain decisions were appropriate to the economic conditions of the textile industry at that time, and others were less critical. By combining the mill data with what is known about factor prices in this period, a strategy for mill survival can be inferred. Mill expansion is consistent with the marked decline in national interest rates in the early twentieth century,

Table 5.1
Comparison of Survivors and Nonsurvivors, at the Industry Level*

	Survivors				Nonsurvivors			
	1885	1900	1910	1919	1885	1900	1910	1919
No. Mills	52	122	221	299	200	208	221	201
Capital (thou$)	733 (38)	413 (107)	468 (199)	552 (260)	345 (107)	320 (159)	355 (186)	450 (168)
Labor	–	530 (92)	504 (166)	544 (218)	–	402 (146)	398 (171)	441 (155)
Capital/Labor	–	852 (83)	928 (151)	1065 (193)	–	797 (119)	904 (147)	1132 (129)
Spindles	46545 (50)	33820 (122)	35371 (219)	33576 (294)	16310 (190)	22788 (203)	25343 (218)	30556 (204)
Ring	–	24749 (80)	29771 (205)	30152 (284)	–	16443 (135)	21453 (214)	26953 (196)
Mule	–	9429 (80)	4741 (205)	3234 (284)	–	7358 (135)	3809 (214)	3486 (196)
Loom	1170 (51)	807 (122)	739 (220)	620 (296)	351 (192)	497 (207)	587 (219)	606 (204)
Population	27629 (44)	29076 (101)	29811 (216)	30648 (297)	14528 (168)	23168 (184)	21604 (216)	26853 (203)
Ring/Spindles	–	.892 (78)	.940 (204)	.962 (279)	–	.841 (123)	.934 (202)	.946 (181)
Electric Power	–	–	.276	.552	–	–	.226	.435
Fine Output	.135	.254	.326	.328	.085	.149	.249	.251
Yarn Only	.135	.361	.425	.488	.290	.380	.443	.498
Age (yrs)	–	8	11	16	–	9	11	16

Source: Compiled by the author from Davison's Textile Blue Book, Official American Textile Directory, for the years cited.
* Number of mills reporting each characteristic shown in parentheses.

which favored capital spending. Rising wages, together with lower interest rates and, in turn, lower rental rates, led to a rising wage-rental rate ratio over the period. The higher rate of adoption of the ring spindle among survivors is consistent with the increase in the wage-rental rate ratio, because of the labor-saving aspect of the ring spindle (see Chapter 4).

The apparent advantage to location in larger cities may stem from proximity to sources of capital, since the financial centers were known to have developed first in the large cities in this period. The use of city population as a proxy for capital availability is suggested by Kenneth L. Sokoloff (1984) in his study of capital investments in manufacturing during the period of early U.S. industrialization. Sokoloff finds that the working capital share of a firm's total investment (the sum of fixed capital and inventories) increased with the degree of urbanization of the county in which the firm was located, with urbanization defined as the proportion of county population that resides in cities of 2,500 or more people (1984, 554–55). Thus a positive association between availability of short-term, working capital and larger cities is consistent with Sokoloff's results. The larger cities also provided a larger local supply of labor. Growth in both the average mill capital and number of employees over the period gives support for either of these explanations, but the evidence does not allow the relative importance of each to be evaluated. The relationship between city size and mill survival will be explored in greater detail.

The relationship between capital intensity, measured by the capital-labor ratio, and mill survival is inconclusive when the industry is examined at the national level. The differences in capital intensity between surviving and nonsurviving mills each year are not great, and the early association of somewhat higher capital intensity with survival breaks down in the last period (in 1919). One explanation for these results is that capital intensity is determined by the regional factor price ratio, and given wide factor price differentials among the U.S. textile producing regions, the profit-maximizing capital intensity varied across mills in the industry. A potential association between capital intensity and mill survival at the regional level is therefore obscured when the mills are examined at the national level.

Age appears to have been a factor in mill survival only in the earlier part of the period. In 1900 mills that were destined to survive to the end of the period were newer compared to mills that eventually failed. Newer mills at the turn of the century had the choice to equip the plant with state-of-the-art spindles and looms, which was likely to give those mills an advantage over older mills that continued to operate with less modern, yet productive, equipment. This advantage was only temporary, however, since the established mills eventually replaced existing machinery with the newest models. By 1910 the older mills (concentrated in the North) were innovating at a faster rate than before, and the surviving mills were no longer distinguishable by age.

DESCRIPTION OF SURVIVORS IN EACH REGION

Next, the surviving mills are analyzed within each region to gain insight into how the survival strategies differed by region and why mills ultimately proved more successful in the South. The statistics for the surviving and nonsurviving mills by region are shown in Table 5.2.

The surviving mills were, on average, larger than nonsurviving mills, based on capital, labor, spindles, ring spindles, and looms. The number of mule spindles was lower for the surviving mills, which also had higher shares of ring spindles, although the difference was small since these shares were so high for all southern mills. Among the surviving mills a larger share used electricity and produced fine output, and a smaller share were specialized spinning mills, compared with the nonsurviving mills. Age was not a factor in survival, probably because most of the southern mills were relatively new.

In the South the average population of mill towns each year was similar for surviving and nonsurviving mills. Mill location in North Carolina probably was not dependent on city size, since none of the cities in that state were large enough to attract financial centers on the order of, say, Charleston, South Carolina, or cities in the North. The largest of the North Carolina populations were less than one-tenth the size of the largest Massachusetts mill cities.

The capital-labor ratio was smaller for the surviving southern mills compared to nonsurviving mills in each year except 1900. The best strategy apparently was to adopt a lower capital intensity than competing mills, because wages were low in the labor-abundant South and rental rates were high, relative to national average factor prices. Because managers operated under uncertainty, varying rates of capital intensity were used in production, and those managers that chose the optimal capital intensity remained in operation. The fact that the capital-labor ratio increased as wages rose in the South supports the hypothesis that mills based capital intensity on prevailing factor prices.

Alternatively, capital-labor ratios could have varied between surviving and nonsurviving mills because local factor prices varied within the South. The surviving mills may have been located where the wage-rental rate ratio was lower than the areas where the nonsurviving mills operated, so that the surviving mills chose lower capital-labor ratios. In that case managements in both groups chose optimal capital intensities in production, but the nonsurviving mills chose the wrong location, where factor prices were less favorable. Another possibility to consider is that the failing mills may have had idle capacity, which would raise their measured capital-labor ratio relative to the surviving mills. Mills with idle capacity may have reported constant capital values as workers were dismissed, raising the capital-labor ratio to higher than the capital intensity used in actual production.

In the North the surviving mills' distinguishing characteristics were size, adoption of the ring spindle, type of output, and size of mill town. The surviving northern mills were consistently larger on average and had a higher capital-labor ratio than the nonsurviving mills. The choice of a more capital-intensive technique generally is consistent with the relatively high wages and low interest rates in the North in this period. A higher capital intensity is not necessarily the best strategy, however, since we lack information about what the optimal capital-intensity was in the North. As in the South, the northern capital intensity in production rose steadily throughout the period, as the wage-rental rate ratio increased.

Table 5.2
Regional Comparison of Surviving and Nonsurviving Mills*

North Carolina	Survivors				Nonsurvivors			
	1885	1900	1910	1919	1885	1900	1910	1919
No. Mills	12	66	148	212	64	107	142	127
Capital (thou$)	154 (6)	143 (59)	202 (135)	246 (184)	62 (26)	100 (82)	147 (122)	189 (103)
Labor	–	226 (48)	265 (108)	292 (148)	–	179 (68)	189 (106)	224 (193)
Capital/Labor	–	804 (43)	830 (98)	983 (130)	–	689 (54)	891 (92)	1122 (77)
Spindles	4139 (12)	7884 (66)	13851 (148)	16157 (211)	3562 (60)	5118 (106)	8873 (142)	11193 (127)
Ring	–	7297 (44)	14070 (140)	16252 (204)	–	5306 (68)	8447 (140)	11226 (121)
Mule	–	0 (44)	100 (140)	87 (204)	–	309 (68)	500 (140)	146 (121)
Loom	86 (12)	175 (66)	260 (148)	237 (212)	49 (62)	118 (107)	140 (142)	159 (127)
Population	1588 (6)	3177 (54)	5617 (144)	5642 (210)	2021 (41)	4142 (91)	5088 (139)	5965 (124)
Ring/Spindles	–	1.000 (42)	.989 (139)	.996 (203)	–	.984 (62)	.976 (135)	.989 (115)
Electric Power	.000	–	.318	.632	–	–	.239	.520
Fine Output	–	.106	.250	.255	.000	.047	.162	.157
Yarn Only	.417	.545	.554	.618	.406	.505	.577	.646
Age (yrs)	–	5	8	13	–	6	7	12

Massachusetts	Survivors				Nonsurvivors			
	1885	1900	1910	1919	1885	1900	1910	1919
No. Mills	40	56	73	87	136	101	79	80
Capital (thou$)	842	745	1030	1291	436	556	752	862
	(32)	(48)	(64)	(76)	(81)	(77)	(64)	(65)
Labor	-	861	949	1077	-	597	738	768
		(44)	(58)	(70)		(78)	(65)	(62)
Capital/Labor	-	904	1108	1234	-	887	927	1146
		(40)	(53)	(63)		(65)	(55)	(52)
Spindles	59937	64386	80229	77858	22194	42096	56116	62492
	(38)	(56)	(71)	(83)	(130)	(97)	(76)	(77)
Ring	-	46080	63590	65595	-	27747	46058	52327
		(36)	(65)	(80)		(67)	(74)	(75)
Mule	-	20954	14737	11258	-	14512	10070	8875
		(36)	(65)	(80)		(67)	(74)	(75)
Loom	1504	1552	1724	1589	495	902	1414	1342
	(39)	(56)	(72)	(84)	(130)	(100)	(77)	(77)
Population	31740	58833	78200	91008	18566	41784	51419	59639
	(38)	(47)	(72)	(87)	(127)	(93)	(77)	(79)
Ring/Spindles	-	.766	.834	.871	-	.696	.848	.872
		(36)	(65)	(76)		(61)	(67)	(66)
Electric Power	-	-	.192	.356	-	-	.203	.300
Fine Output	.175	.429	.479	.506	.125	.257	.405	.400
Yarn Only	.050	.143	.164	.172	.235	.248	.203	.263
Age (yrs)	-	12	17	23	-	12	18	22

Source: Compiled by the author from Davison's Textile Blue Book, Official American Textile Directory, for the years cited.

Prior to 1910 adoption of the ring spindle was apparently linked to survival in the North. In each year of directories sampled between 1895 and 1905, the ratio of ring spindles to total spindles was higher among surviving northern mills than nonsurviving mills (only the statistics in 1900, not 1895 or 1905, are reported in Table 5.2). The association disappears after 1910, when mills in both groups had raised the share of ring spindles to well over 80 percent of total spindle stock.

The share of mills producing fine output was higher for surviving northern mills compared to nonsurvivors, which supports the popular view that northern mills competed with the southern industry by turning to successively higher grades of textile output in this period. That strategy apparently was important to the survival of the northern branch of the industry until the southern mills entered the fine-output markets in the 1920s.

The surviving northern mills were located in larger mill towns than the nonsurviving mills. The advantage of location in the larger mill towns in the North may have stemmed from greater access either to capital or to labor. As discussed earlier, the city population can be a proxy for capital availability, because the financial centers were first established in the larger cities. A larger population may also imply a larger labor supply for the mills. In particular the supply of immigrant labor was likely to have been greater in the larger cities in the North. Immigrants formed a large share of the northern mill labor force in this period, so proximity to that population would have been important in the North.

SURVIVAL WITHIN CITIES

The next stage of analysis compares surviving and failing mills within the same city. Focusing on individual cities allows locational factors that might have determined mill survival, such as local factor prices, quality of the labor force, and local taxes to remain constant. Assuming that the mills in one locality were subject to the same external operating conditions, analyzing survival within cities will reveal what attributes besides location, if any, are associated with mill survival.

Some factors that were likely to vary for mills within the same city and that may have been important for mill survival include mill size, type of spindles used, firm structure (whether specialized or integrated), and type of yarn or cloth produced. Parameters that depended on factor prices, such as the capital-labor ratio, would have been identical for all mills if all faced the same local wages and interest rates, although no evidence supports that assertion. But since the capital-labor ratio depends on both input prices and management efficiency, observed differences in capital-labor ratios could be explained by local variation in either set of factors.

Mills were segregated on the basis of their population values, which usually were unique for each mill town within the region. In cases where mill towns were known to have had the same total population, the original entries were used to separate mills into the proper city groups. Within each city, surviving and nonsurviving mills were compared on the basis of average capital, average capital-labor ratio, and average ring-spindle ratio. Table 5.3 summarizes the results of the analysis of survival in the mill towns where both surviving and failing mills were located. Statistics are reported for two selected years, 1885 and 1910.

A sizable share of mills in each region were located in one-mill towns in both periods, so were not included in Table 5.3. In North Carolina about one-third of mills in 1885 were the only mill in town, and the share drops to one-fifth by 1910. As noted above, southern towns generally were small and scattered in that region, so the prevalence of single-mill towns in the South is not surprising. That one-fifth of mills in Massachusetts were in one-mill towns in both periods was unexpected, however. The relatively large mill towns of the North at that time seem likely to have supported more than one mill. Moreover, the advantages of agglomeration, which Hekman (1980) and Hekman and Strong (1981) have suggested was an early advantage to location in the North, would have led to a higher degree of mill concentration in the northern mill towns than we find in the mill directory evidence.[3]

The analysis in this section requires information about both surviving and nonsurviving mills that operated in the same city.

In North Carolina a small share of total mills were located in cities that had both types of mills, however. In 1885 only 9 percent of mills, and in 1910, 47 percent of mills fit this description in North Carolina. The remaining mills were located in cities hosting only one mill or only one type of mill, surviving or nonsurviving. A larger share of mills in Massachusetts could be compared on the basis of survival within the same city, since 48 percent of all mills in 1885 and 68 percent in 1910 were located where both surviving and nonsurviving mills existed.

As shown in Table 5.3, the northern mills tended to be concentrated in a few large cities (New Bedford, Lowell, and Fall River), whereas southern mills were fairly evenly distributed across the mill cities included in the table. The contrast in the geographic distribution of mills in the two regions in these data is consistent with the generalization that southern mills were smaller, more numerous, and more widely dispersed than those in the North before 1930.

Table 5.3
Mill Survival, by City: 1885 and 1910

1885 Population	Survivors No.	Survivors Capital	Nonsurvivors No.	Nonsurvivors Capital
		North Carolina		
35	1	$250,000	1	$85,000
817	1	--	4	25,000
		Massachusetts		
4030	1	400,000	1	--
4053	2	200,000	2	200,000
5504	1	800,000	2	400,000
5591	1	--	2	785,000
12,429	1	--	3	75,000
21,213	1	600,000	7	111,667
21,915	1	500,000	3	710,000
26,845	3	1,666,667	2	150,000
39,151	3	1,083,333	4	1,112,500
48,961	14	550,769	24	446,864
59,475	3	1,733,333	4	13,500,000

Table 5.3 (continued)

1910

Population	No.	Survivors Capital	K/L[a]	R/S[b]	No.	Nonsurvivors Capital	K/L[a]	R/S[b]
				North Carolina				
300	2	$ 87,500	575	1	1	$105,000	--	1
520	1	200,000	--	1	1	--	--	1
600	1	45,000	563	1	1	50,000	1000	1
615	1	120,000	--	--	2	65,750	583	1
850	1	110,000	--	1	2	187,500	1292	1
1,000	2	87,500	--	1	1	65,700	438	1
1,200	(a) 2	87,375	623	1	3	43,333	540	1
	(b) 1	90,000	--	1	2	125,000	1200	1
1,500	(a) 7	225,000	691	1	1	375,000	750	1
	(b) 1	73,000	365	1	1	40,800	453	1
1,900	3	101,250	545	1	1	98,181	818	--
2,000	(a) 3	105,267	831	1	2	87,350	994	1
	(b) 2	530,000	480	1	2	35,450	444	1
	(c) 4	101,813	645	1	4	92,750	1064	1
2,500	1	228,000	380	1	1	100,000	1250	1
3,000	2	65,900	1060	1	6	101,983	1111	1
3,100	1	290,000	967	1	3	63,333	560	1
3,540	1	--	--	1	3	77,333	256	1
4,620	3	162,667	1085	1	2	146,000	679	1
4,700	4	76,000	623	1	4	158,750	998	1
5,000	5	215,960	811	1	1	30,000	100	1
6,030	6	167,533	1153	1	6	317,467	867	1
9,000	1	100,000	--	1	1	240,000	960	1
10,000	2	428,000	721	1	8	174,167	1000	1
12,500	1	250,000	556	1	3	121,667	711	1
25,000	1	150,000	545	1	3	227,333	1160	.667
26,755	1	250,000	500	1	1	250,000	1667	--
43,000	4	730,025	971	1	6	206,250	1444	1
				Massachusetts				
1,500	1	$ --	--	.895	1	$ 675,000	1125	1
4,450	1	--	--	.534	2	--	--	1
14,000	2	40,000	320	1	2	1,850,000	1143	.735
31,036	1	1,000,000	909	.922	5	186,000	855	.800
31,531	2	350,000	1120	1	4	300,000	770	.922
45,712	1	--	--	--	3	765,000	780	.851
62,559	3	1,250,000	642	1	2	4,700,000	718	1
94,969	2	2,700,000	987	.780	6	1,181,667	988	.771
100,000	20	1,263,000	1310	.691	3	1,383,333	1333	.612
104,863	23	802,500	1149	.898	16	787,606	969	.867
560,892	1	1,250,000	--	1	1	--	--	--

Source: Compiled by the author from Davison's Textile Blue Book, Official American Textile Directory.

[a] K/L=capital/labor

[b] R/S=ring spindles/total spindles

Little information is found for 1885 from the southern cities with both surviving and failing mills, since only two cities fell into this category. By 1910 there were twenty-eight cities with both surviving and nonsurviving mills, and in about one-third of these, either the capital or capital-labor ratio was similar between the two types of mills. This result lends support to the assumption that mills faced the same factor prices within a city, which would lead managements to choose similar profit-maximizing input ratios. All southern mills in these cities used the ring spindle exclusively, which is consistent with the very high reliance on that type of spindle in the region. Based on these selected variables, surviving mills are not easily distinguished from those destined to fail before 1930 within the same city. Some other factor that has not been reported here may have been important in determining mill survival in the South.

The comparison of surviving and nonsurviving northern mills by city produces even stronger support for the hypothesis that mills chose a similar capital level and capital intensity within a city, where all mills pay the same local factor prices. Since northern mills tended to be concentrated in the larger cities, there are more mills to be studied in the northern cities reported in Table 5.3. In the larger northern cities, the average capital value and capital-labor ratios of each category of mill are strikingly similar on a city-by-city basis.

In 1910 evidence about the type of spindle used tends to distinguish surviving from nonsurviving mills. That year the share of ring spindles in total spindles was usually higher among surviving northern mills compared with those that failed in the same city. In cities with 85 percent of the mills listed in Table 5.3 that year, the ring share was higher among the surviving mills than mills that failed. The type of spindle used appears to have played a role in mill survival in the North, but mill size and capital intensity of production apparently were not related to survival within the same city. The analysis of mills partitioned by city provides evidence about the importance of the ring spindle that is consistent with similar findings reported in the earlier investigation of mill survival conducted at the industry and regional levels.

NOTES

1. There were thirteen mills affected by mergers in the Massachusetts sample and twenty-one mergers in the North Carolina group. Without information about the financial status of these mills prior to the mergers, it is uncertain whether it is correct to treat these mills as nonsurvivors. The number of mills involved are few, however, so a bias resulting from misclassifying these mills would be small.

2. Increasing economies of scale are now achieved at a mill size of up to 10,000 spindles and continue at a lessened pace up to 20,000 spindles, at which economies of scale are then exhausted (UNIDO 1969, 70).

3. The benefits of agglomeration, or the clustering of firms in an area, result from being close to other firms in the same and related industries (Hekman and Strong 1981, 35).

6

Probability of Mill Survival

LOGISTIC REGRESSION

The descriptive analysis of the mills surviving to 1930 in the textile industry presented in Chapter 5 provides the basis for linking mill strategies to longevity in the industry. Regression analysis of the probability of mill survival to 1930 provides a statistical measure of the association between various mill attributes and mill survival. The model to be estimated is based on a relationship between a binary dependent variable, the choice between survival or failure, and several independent variables that consist of several mill characteristics. Since the dependent variable is not continuous, but is rather a discrete variable that takes on the values one or zero, the special models of qualitative choice are appropriate for regression analysis.[1]

In particular a logit model is used to study the event of mill survival (or failure). The logit model overcomes certain statistical problems of dealing with a binary dependent variable by estimating the odds that a particular choice will be made, rather than the binary variable or the probability of that choice. In other words, the dependent variable in a logit model is $[p/(1-p)]$, rather than $[p]$, where $[p]$ represents the probability of an event. Information from the regression estimation of the logit dependent variable (the odds of an event or choice occurring) can be used to learn about the probability of that event through simple calculations.

Mill survival was probably associated with the mill features that were recorded in the mill directories, because of the underlying relationship between the mill characteristics and unobserved factor prices in each region. Mill survival is assumed to be a function of rational, profit-maximizing decisions about textile production, based on information about factor prices and product prices. Since these prices were not reported by the individual mills, however, the parameters of mill production instead must reveal the source for mill survival in each region.

The logit model transforms the functional relationship between the dummy variable for survival and the various mill characteristics to the estimation of:

$$\ln[\, p/(1-p)] = X_i\beta_i + u, \tag{1}$$

where $\ln$ = natural logarithm, p = probability of mill survival, X_i = vector of mill characteristics, β_i = vector of coefficients, and u = error term. The expression on the left can be interpreted as the odds of survival occurring, rather than the probability of survival. Thus the logit model creates a dependent variable that can span the range of the entire real line, as opposed to the interval that the probability must fall within, between zero and one.

The range of estimates of the parameters β resulting from the regressions can indicate the direction of association between the particular mill characteristic and the probability of mill survival, holding all other characteristics constant. This allows one to isolate a mill characteristic and analyze the pairwise association between that variable and mill survival. The results of the regression using the logit model for mill data in each region in 1900 are presented in Table 6.1. The parameters of the model were estimated by the Maximum Likelihood method, using a Newton-Raphson algorithm.

To get an indication of how sensitive the regression estimates are to variations in the model specification, five versions of the logit model for the probability of mill survival were tested.[2] The sign and statistical significance of an estimate will have

Table 6.1
Logit Models of Probability of Mill Survival in 1900

			Models		
	(1)	(2)	(3)	(4)	(5)

North Carolina

	(1)	(2)	(3)	(4)	(5)
Intercept	-11.74	-11.75	-11.74	-1.42	-12.14
Capital	-6×10^{-8}			1×10^{-6}	-1×10^{-7}
Spindles		8×10^{-7}			
KOL	2×10^{-4}	2×10^{-4}	2×10^{-4}		2×10^{-4}
ROS[a]					
POP	-8×10^{-5}*	-8×10^{-5}*	-8×10^{-5}*	-6×10^{-5}*	-8×10^{-5}*
DPS	12.41	12.40	12.40	1.60	12.53
FINE	.41	.41	.41	1.04	.50
YROLD	-.10*	-.10*	-.10*	-.07	
YROLDSQ					-.01
Likelihood Ratio	59.67*	62.45*	59.68*	87.20**	60.67*

Massachusetts

	(1)	(2)	(3)	(4)	(5)
Intercept	-6.29	-6.70	-6.32	-14.58	-6.74
Capital	7×10^{-7}			8×10^{-7}	7×10^{-7}
Spindles		5×10^{-6}			
KOL	3×10^{-4}	1×10^{-3}	1×10^{-3}		4×10^{-4}
ROS	3.08*	3.13*	2.84*	3.68**	3.15*
POP	4×10^{-5}***	4×10^{-5}***	4×10^{-5}***	4×10^{-5}***	4×10^{-5}***
DPS[a]					
FINE	2.21***	2.24***	2.30***	2.28***	2.28***
YROLD	-.05	-.04	-.03	-.04	
YROLDSQ					-2×10^{-3}
Likelihood Ratio	59.08	60.57	61.29	66.90	59.48

[a] Variable had a value of one for all mills in the regression.
* p = .10, ** p = .05, *** p = .01

greater credibility if the results are consistent across variations in the model, so that a particular result is not unique to the set of independent variables that the researcher has perhaps arbitrarily decided to include in the model.

The independent variables listed on the left in Table 6.1 indicate the mill characteristics that were included in the five models. The basic model for the probability of mill survival includes measures of mill size, capital intensity, share of ring spindles in total spindles, city population, type of power used, type of output, and mill age. Since all of the descriptions of mill size found in the directories—capital, employees, spindles and looms—were highly correlated, just one of these was chosen to proxy mill size in any version of the model. Mill size is expected to be positively associated with mill survival in each region, primarily because of economies of scale in mill production.

The direction of the association of capital intensity, measured by the capital-labor ratio (KOL), with survival is uncertain. Capital intensity depends on both local factor prices and the choice of textile production technique, between the mule or ring spindle, and the standard or automatic loom. In the high-wage North the optimal choice for KOL would have been higher than in the South. It is difficult to compare capital intensity among mills in the same region, however, without information about the optimal capital intensity. In either region a firm will be more likely to be profitable, the closer the capital intensity of production is to the optimal capital intensity; KOL either above or below the optimal level will impair a mill's chances for survival. Increases in KOL will be positively associated with survival up to the point where the optimal KOL is achieved, and negatively associated thereafter. Without the optimal KOL in each region as a point of reference, however, the expected association between KOL and survival is uncertain.

Capital intensity was also determined in part by the choice of machinery used in production, since the capital value of the relatively newer spindle and loom models was approximately three times that of the older models for an equal spindle or loom capacity. Based on the hypothesis that the superiority of the new machinery—the ring spindle and the automatic loom—contributed to mill survival, a positive association between KOL and mill survival is expected in both regions, stemming from use of the new machinery.

The ring-spindle ratio (ROS) is a proxy for the adoption of technological improvements in textile machinery in this period.

ROS is expected to be positively associated with survival. Historians often referred to the use of modern equipment among the southern mills as an important advantage in competition with the North (Mitchell 1921, 246). Use of the ring was reported to have reduced variable costs in production, due to savings in labor costs, which would have led to a higher profit margin and, therefore, survival for those innovating mills.

Population (POP) is a proxy for the availability of capital and labor, which were possibly more accessible in the larger towns. A larger value for POP indirectly promotes a larger mill size, through reduced restrictions on the supply of either capital or labor, and thus leads to a positive association with survival. Besides the advantages of greater local factor supplies, the large towns may have offered economies of agglomeration that would attract mills. In a large town a mill would be near other mills to learn industry news more quickly, machine shops to facilitate repairs, suppliers to reduce the distance raw materials are shipped, and the commission houses that marketed the textile products.

The dummy variable for the use of the modern source of power, steam (DPS), instead of the water wheel, is expected to be an indication of mills with an innovative and farsighted management, and, therefore, a greater chance of survival. The dummy variable for fine output, FINE, is expected to be relevant to mill survival in the North, where mills apparently strategically shifted to the production of fine output as the southern mills became competitive in the lower grades of output.

The variable YROLD is the number of years the mill has been in operation, based on the earliest directory in which the mill appears in this data set. YROLDSQ is the square of the years-old variable. Both YROLD and YROLDSQ are expected to be negatively related to survival, since the mills established in the nineteenth century were less likely to have installed the improved machinery initially, so were handicapped with obsolete spindles and looms until the equipment wore out. YROLDSQ is anticipated to emphasize the disadvantage of the earliest mills, by introducing the quadratic term. Perhaps YROLDSQ will capture the nonlinear relationship between age and survival, since it was found that the new and oldest mills, at the extreme in the age distribution, had lower survival rates than the middle-aged mills each year (recall Table 4.5).

The five versions of the regression model experiment with excluding some of the above variables, one at a time. Model (1) includes all variables and uses capital to measure mill size. Model (2) substitutes spindles for capital, which may be a more accurate measure of mill capacity. Model (3) eliminates the variable for size, which may be valid if there were no significant economies of scale in textile production or if rental rates did not vary significantly between regions. Model (4) eliminates the variable for capital intensity and thus focuses on the level of factor prices and their effect on products, not factor price ratios. Model (5) substitutes the quadratic term YROLDSQ for YROLD, and is expected to better approximate the relationship between age and survival. The variables ROS, POP, DPS, and FINE are included in all five versions of the logit model.

REGRESSION RESULTS

The regression estimates suggest that southern and northern mills operating in 1900 took different strategies to survive. In the South survival was associated with smaller mill towns and newer mills, compared with the mills that had failed by 1930 in that region. Both the population and age coefficients were negative and statistically significant at the 10 percent level.

The unexpected inverse relationship between town size and mill survival may be explained by the advantages of the "mill town," where the mill owned the housing, stores, school, and church. A mill town was more likely to be a less populous city, and the greater degree of control over the mill labor force in those places may have contributed to mill survival.[3] Although the larger cities were expected to be better sources of capital and labor, it may be that even the largest North Carolina cities at this time were still too small to attract significantly greater factor supplies than the smaller southern towns. The negative association between age and survival supports the hypothesis that the older mills were at a disadvantage, since newer mills could innovate sooner than mills with operable machinery that had usable lifetimes remaining.

Unfortunately, there was not enough variation in the ROS variable among southern mills for any statistical correlation with the probability of survival. Such a large proportion of southern mills used ring spindles exclusively by 1900 that ROS was one for all but one of the mills reporting the type of spindle used in the directories that year. Another problem encountered in measuring the role of the ring spindle in mill survival is that 45 percent of the southern mills failed to report in the 1900 directory whether ring or mule spindles were used.

In the North mill survival was associated with a higher share of ring spindles, a larger mill-town population, and the production of fine output. The measure of the adoption of the ring spindle in the northern mills, ROS, had a positive and statistically significant coefficient. There was wider diversity in the use of the ring spindle in the northern mills in 1900 than in the southern mills, which provides enough information to test the role of that innovation in the northern textile industry. Although data on production costs is lacking to investigate why the ring spindle provided northern mills with a competitive advantage in that region, the suggestion of a relationship between the new technology and mill longevity supports the hypothesis that technological change had an important impact on the textile industry.

The population estimate was positive and statistically significant in the North, which supports the notion that the larger cities provided greater access to financial capital and labor, but could also indicate that there were agglomeration economies. The positive and statistically significant association between fine output and survival is consistent with a northern strategy to compete with the southern mills by shifting to higher grades of product. Those northern mills that specialized in lower grades of output competed directly with mills in the South that had the advantages of lower wages and more modern machinery, and the regression results do not contradict this view.

ELASTICITIES

The magnitude of the relationship between the independent variables and mill survival can be measured by the elasticity of the probability of mill survival with respect to changes in each of the mill characteristics. The elasticity E_{p,X_i} indicates the percentage change in p for a 1 percent change in X_i. The range of elasticities found in Table 6.2 have been calculated according to:

$$E_{p,X_i} = \beta_i X_i (1 - p), \tag{2}$$

where β_i is the vector of regression coefficients. Equation (2) was derived using the logistic cumulative density function:

$$p = 1/[1 + \exp(-X_i\beta_i)]$$

and

$$dp/dX_i = \beta_i \exp(-X_i\beta_i)/[1 + exp(-X_i\beta_i)]^2$$

so that

$$
\begin{aligned}
(dp/dX_i)(X_i/p) &= \{\beta_i exp(-X_i\beta_i)/[1 + exp(-X_i\beta_i)]^2\}(X_i/p) \\
&= p^2\beta_i exp(-X_i\beta_i)X_i/p \\
&= p\beta_i[(1/p) - 1]X_i \\
&= \beta_i X_i(1 - p).
\end{aligned}
$$

The elasticities are evaluated at the means of the independent variables, X_i, and at $p = 0.5$. The minimum and maximum values for the elasticities are reported for each region in Table 6.2, based on the regression estimates that were reported in Table 6.1. Where the range of the estimated elasticity spans zero, the hypothesis that there is no relationship between the variable and survival cannot be rejected. In those cases the regression estimate and the elasticity estimate are sensitive to the choice of included variables in the model, and little confidence can be placed in the results.

In the South it appears that mill age, mill-town population, type of power used, and capital intensity had the biggest impact on the chances of mill survival. Only the first two estimates were statistically significant in the regression, however. In the North the share of ring spindles, population, and type of output had the highest elasticities, which are the same vari-

Table 6.2
Elasticities of Probability of Mill Survival in 1900
(Minimum and Maximum Values, $p = 0.5$)

Variable	North Carolina		Massachusetts	
	Mean	Elasticity	Mean	Elasticity
Capital($)	117,865	-.01 to .08	628,408	.22 to .24
Spindles	6,180	.002	50,255	.12
KOL	740	.07 to .15	893	.17 to .38
ROS	.990	--	.722	1.03 to 1.33
POP	3,783	-.16 to -.12	47,508	.84 to .90
DPS	.919	.73 to 5.76	.936	--
FINE	.069	.01 to .04	.318	.35 to .37
YROLD	5.32	-.28 to -.19	11.56	-.31 to -.18
YROLDSQ	59.54	-.16	161.94	-.15

ables that had statistically significant estimates in the regressions. The elasticity estimates generally corroborate the regression findings. The estimates were sensitive to the model choice only in the case of the variable capital in the southern mill data.

MISSING VALUES

The previous regressions included only those mills that had complete observations for all of the variables that appeared in the regression models. The exclusion of mills with missing values for one or more mill characteristics that were collected from the mill directories may have created a problem, if ignoring those mills introduced a bias to the regression results. A bias may result if the excluded mills were different, on average, from the mills included in the regression analysis. In this section those mills for which the directory entries were incomplete are examined to be aware of any potential bias imposed by excluding those cases.

The problem of missing values was especially acute in the logit regression of mills operating in 1900. At that time only one-third of all the mills listed in the directories had complete information about the variables that were included in the regression model used here. Although the full data set was useful in calculating the regional statistics that were reported in Chapter 5, the number of mills included in the regressions was dramatically less than the total number that were listed in the directories.

Almost all of the excluded mills lacked information about capital or labor, so that the capital-labor ratio (KOL) could not be calculated. The mills that were missing values for KOL tended to be smaller than the average in each region. Among the southern mills missing KOL values, the average survival rate was about 8 percentage points lower than the average for all southern mills in 1900, and northern mills missing KOL had a lower average survival rate by about 5 percentage points than the average northern mill that year. These rough comparisons suggest that missing observations led to the exclusion of mills that were somewhat smaller and less likely to succeed than the average mill in each region in the 1900 regressions. Adding these cases to the regression most likely would have supported the general conclusions of the analysis, however. The positive association between mill size and survival in the regressions is consistent with the pattern found among those mills missing values for KOL, where size and survival were both lower than regional averages.

An attempt was made to include those mills for which capital or labor values were missing by substituting the regional average values for these two variables, known as the "zero-order regression" method of handling the problem of missing observations (Maddala 1977, 202). These cases were then identified with a dummy variable indicating that the mill had missing value(s). The dummy variable allows one to test whether the intercept of a regression based on the group of mills with missing values is different from the intercept for a separate regression based on the rest of the mills. This still leaves the possibility that the two groups have significantly different regression slopes, even though their intercepts are equal, however.

The logistic regression results, using model (5), showed that the estimate of the coefficient of the missing value dummy was not significant. In spite of the fact that a large proportion of mills were excluded from the regression of mills operating in 1900, inclusion of those mills apparently would not have significantly altered the intercept in the estimate of the regression.

It is also unlikely that the slopes of the regressions would have been changed by including the group of mills with missing observations. For the regression slopes to be different in an estimate based on the mills with missing values, those mills would have to vary systematically from the other mills, with the differences widening at either the lower or higher values of the independent variables. Statistical analysis of the mills with missing values revealed the same pattern of association between mill size and the rate of survival as in the rest of the sample of mills. The slope of the regression is unlikely to have been affected by excluding mills with missing observations, since those mills probably would have supported the correlations found between mill survival and the various characteristics among the mills without the missing-values problem.

SPINDLE GROWTH

In the previous sections the progress of the textile industry in each region was analyzed by separating mills into two distinct groups, survivors and nonsurvivors. Survival was defined as simply remaining in operation, and financially healthy mills were not differentiated from financially weak ones. Here an attempt is made to refine the study of mill survivorship by investigating the factors that led to the expansion of the industry in each region, rather than simply mill survival. Industry expansion is measured here by the growth in mill spindles in each decade during the period 1900 to 1930.

The direction and magnitude of growth in spindle capacity perhaps better describes the dynamics of the relocation of the textile industry in this period than did the logit analysis of mill survival. The relocation was a process of both mill failure and a slowdown in additions to mill capacity in the North. As indicated in Tables 3.2 and 3.6, the northern textile industry continued to expand through the 1920s in terms of both number of mills and mill capacity. The shift of production to the South was indicated by a much faster rate of growth in total spindles compared with the North, rather than an absolute decline in the northern industry (up to the mid-1920s).

In fact, the average rate of growth in spindles among the mills in each region was much greater in the South than in the

Table 6.3
Spindle Growth, by Region
(Percent per Decade)

	Year	Avg.	Min.	Max.
North Carolina	1910	92.5%	-49.5%	748.5%
	1919	36.0	-27.9	337.5
	1930	38.6	-100.0	1500.0
Massachusetts	1910	30.2	-48.8	360.0
	1919	9.7	-50.0	140.3
	1930	2.3	-100.0	333.1

Source: Compiled by the author from Davison's Textile Blue Book and Official American Textile Directory.

North in 1910, 1919, and 1930, based on directory evidence (see Table 6.3). Moreover, the average rate of growth of spindles among the northern mills declined steadily over that period. The southern average growth of spindles also dropped in 1919, but picked up slightly by 1930.

The determinants of spindle growth are investigated here by linear regression methods, where the dependent (left-side) variable is the rate of growth in each mill's total number of spindles over the previous decade. Spindle growth is calculated as the percentage change in the number of spindles from the beginning to the end of each decade, using the beginning spindle stock as the base. For example, spindle growth in 1910 is the increase in spindles from 1900 to 1910, divided by the 1900 level of spindles. Three sets of regressions were estimated, at 1910, 1919, and 1930, separately for each region.

Expansion of mill capacity is taken here as a sign of a mill's success, in lieu of information about each mill's profits and market share. Additions to capacity require sufficient funding, whether from retained earnings or external sources, and prospects for future earnings to justify the investment in mill equipment. Since additions to mill capacity may be a sign of mill health, the model of spindle growth is thought to be similar to that of mill survival. The same set of mill characteristics that were included in the logit models of mill survival reappear in these regression models of spindle growth. As in the previous section, factor prices, technological changes, and other unobserved conditions are understood to be the underlying forces that explain mill profitability and success, whether success is measured by mill survival or growth in spindles. The mill characteristics that are observed reflect management choices, which are assumed to have been based on profit-maximizing decisions.

As with most proxy variables, spindle growth is not a perfect substitute for measures of mill profitability, however. Although failing mills are not likely to invest in additional mill equipment, profitable mills will not necessarily choose to expand mill capacity. A mill that currently operates at an optimum scale may decide to make other forms of investment rather than widen its scale of operations. Thus a profitable mill might, in theory, report no spindle growth. Another consideration is that mills could expand mill output by running multiple shifts without increasing plant equipment. Since mills reported equipment stocks only, not utilization rates or number of shifts, spindle growth may not be directly related to mill production. This introduces another weakness in the assumed relationship between spindle growth and expansion of a mill's market share.

The simple methodology of considering net changes in spindle capacity over each decade also masks underlying outlays on mill equipment. In theory a mill might make three different types of outlays on spindles (Stanback 1969, 9). Modernization outlays would replace existing spindles with new models that reduce variable costs at the same level of output. Simple replacement outlays would also maintain the same level of capacity but would not generate the production-cost savings. A third type of investment would be expansion of capacity to increase total output, without reducing variable costs. In practice investment in mill spindles is likely to be some combination of these three categories of outlays. Judging from the statistical description of the mill data that was presented in Chapter 3, mills typically chose to modernize as well as to expand production capacity in this period. Growth in total spindles was affected, as well as a switch from mule to ring spindles in both

Table 6.4
Linear Models of Spindle Growth, by Region:
1910, 1919, and 1930

1910	(1)	Models (2)	(3)
North Carolina (83 mills)			
Intercept	-.407	-1.161	-.087
CAPITAL	5×10^{-5}*		
SPINDLES		6×10^{-5}*	
KOL	-3×10^{-4}	3×10^{-4}	1×10^{-4}
ROS	1.383	1.539*	1.267
DPE	.269	.295	.215
POP	6×10^{-6}	-1×10^{-5}	3×10^{-5}
DOUTFINE	-.592	-.100	-.093
YROLDSQ	-.002*	-.001*	-.001*
R^2	.348	.450	.160
Massachusetts (83 mills)			
Intercept	.321	.304	.255
CAPITAL	2×10^{-7}		
SPINDLES		8×10^{-6}*	
KOL	-1×10^{-4}	-8×10^{-5}	-7×10^{-5}
ROS	.147	.067	.199
DPE	.099	.061	.117
POP	-7×10^{-6}	-1×10^{-5}	-6×10^{-6}
DOUTFINE	.060	.074	.050
YROLDSQ	-2×10^{-4}	-2×10^{-4}	-2×10^{-4}
R^2	.040	.074	.035

regions. To the extent mill expansion was accomplished through modernization, lower variable costs and higher profitability may have been achieved.

With those caveats noted, the linear regression of spindle growth in each region can be studied. The independent variables that are included in the regression models of spindle growth are listed in the left-hand column in Table 6.4. Both CAPITAL and SPINDLES are included as measures of mill size,

Table 6.4 (continued)

1919	(1)	Models (2)	(3)
North Carolina (155 mills)			
Intercept	.321	.304	.255
CAPITAL	2×10^{-7}		
SPINDLES		$8 \times 10^{-6}*$	
KOL	-1×10^{-4}	-8×10^{-5}	-7×10^{-5}
ROS	.147	.067	.199
DPE	.099	.061	.117
POP	-7×10^{-6}	-1×10^{-5}	-6×10^{-6}
DOUTFINE	.060	.074	.050
YROLDSQ	-2×10^{-4}	-2×10^{-4}	-2×10^{-4}
R^2	.040	.074	.035
Massachusetts (95 mills)			
Intercept	.179	.110	.126
CAPITAL	3×10^{-8}		
SPINDLES		$2 \times 10^{-6}*$	
KOL	-2×10^{-5}	7×10^{-7}	7×10^{-6}
ROS	.086	.123	.105
DPE	.049	.025	.056
POP	-8×10^{-7}	$-2 \times 10^{-6}*$	-7×10^{-7}
DOUTFINE	-.030	-.032	-.019
YROLDSQ	-1×10^{-4}	$-1 \times 10^{-4}*$	-1×10^{-4}
R^2	.087	.137	.066

and the coefficients for these two variables are expected to be positive. Spindle growth is expected to be directly related to mill size, because an increase in capacity requires capital to finance the purchase of new spindles. In addition, if mill size contributes to mill profitability, perhaps because of economies of scale, a larger mill size may raise the prospect of future profits to warrant expansion in mill capacity.

The level of capital intensity, KOL, may be associated with spindle growth in a number of ways. Technological innovation may provide an indirect link between KOL and spindle growth.

Table 6.4 (continued)

1930	(1)	Models (2)	(3)
North Carolina (135 mills)			
Intercept	199.636	195.115	197.759
CAPITAL	-2×10^{-8}		
SPINDLES		2×10^{-6}	
KOL	-5×10^{-5}	-6×10^{-5}	-5×10^{-5}
ROS	-199.168	-194.666	-197.284
DPE	.149	.134	.145
POP	-2×10^{-6}	-3×10^{-6}	-2×10^{-6}
DOUTFINE	-.075	-.065	-.074
YROLDSQ	-3×10^{-4}*	-3×10^{-4}*	-3×10^{-4}*
R^2	.109	.116	.108
Massachusetts (55 mills)			
Intercept	-.208	-.353	-.139
CAPITAL	6×10^{-8}		
SPINDLES		2×10^{-6}*	
KOL	-1×10^{-4}	-8×10^{-5}	-6×10^{-5}
ROS	.143	.237	.053
DPE	.147	.166	.177
POP	-2×10^{-7}	-4×10^{-7}	-2×10^{-7}
DOUTFINE	.211*	.173	.199
YROLDSQ	-1×10^{-5}	-3×10^{-5}	3×10^{-6}
R^2	.192	.232	.167

* The t-statistic was at least 2.0.

Adoption of modern equipment would have raised the capital-labor ratio because of the higher prices of the new machinery, which were about triple the prices of the standard equipment. Since capital intensity is measured here by the value of capital stock, rising equipment prices would raise KOL even if the number of machines was kept constant. The labor-saving aspect of the new technology would have contributed to a higher capital intensity, by reducing the amount of labor required per unit of capital. In addition, to the extent innovation raised mill productivity, by increasing output per spindle, spindle growth would rise in response to improved mill profitability. Finally, factor prices affected KOL and spindle growth. Where the wage-rental rate ratio was high, in the North, mills would substitute capital for labor and raise KOL to some optimal level. The optimal level of KOL would have been lower in the South, because the wage-rental rate ratio was lower there. Across mills within each region, levels of KOL that were closer to the optimal level would be associated with profitability and spindle growth. As noted above, though, information is lacking about what that optimal level of KOL was each period, so the expected association between KOL and spindle growth is uncertain.

Adoption of the ring spindle, measured by ROS, is expected to contribute to mill profitability because of the labor-saving advantage to producing with a ring rather than a mule spindle. Thus ROS and spindle growth would be positively associated, to the extent spindle growth reflects a mill's current and expected future profitability. Use of the ring spindle may also promote a higher level of spindle capacity, because the same number of employees can operate more spindles compared with a mill equipped with mule spindles.

The adoption of electricity, indicated by the dummy variable DPE, may signal the innovative and successful managements, which also would have promoted mill profitability and spindle growth. The use of electricity as opposed to only steam boilers or water wheels could have removed the constraints on mill size that may have been imposed on the older types of power sources. In addition, electricity was associated with operating night shifts, which probably boosted mill profits by reducing the average cost of production.

The production of fine output, measured by FINE, was thought to have been a competitive strategy in the North as southern mills gradually dominated textile production by grade of output. Thus FINE and spindle growth are expected to be positively related for the northern branch of the industry. So few southern mills produced fine output that little association between these two variables is expected in the South, however.

The last variable included in the models, YROLDSQ, estimates mill age, which is squared to reflect the more than proportionate effect of mill age on mill performance. The impact of mill age on spindle growth is uncertain. Older mills may have been less likely to expand, either because their equipment was obsolete and placed them at a competitive disadvantage, or because they were replacing, rather than supplementing, mill capacity. Older mills may have reached an optimal plant size and maintained, rather than expanded, mill capacity in this period. On the other hand, older mills might have been expanding more rapidly than newer mills because, as noted in earlier sections, the oldest mills had among the highest survival rates in the industry. The data showed that the older mills were more likely than newer mills to have converted to using the ring spindle, which may have contributed to mill profitability and survival, and in turn, spindle growth.

The regression results are reported in Table 6.4. In both regions spindle growth was found to have been associated with mill size and age. The estimates of the coefficients for CAPITAL and SPINDLES were positive and often statistically significant for both northern and southern mills throughout the period 1900 to 1930. Although the reasons for the apparent advantage of a larger mill size than other mills in a region are not clear from this analysis, it is possible that economies of scale in production or greater access to factor supplies in the labor and capital markets may have been important.

Mill age, indicated by YROLDSQ, may have been negatively associated with spindle growth. In both regions the estimate of the coefficient for YROLDSQ was frequently negative and statistically significant. This lends support for the hypothesis that the oldest mills were burdened with less modern and older equipment, which may have reduced their profitability. However, in this study, data are lacking on the vintage of mill equipment. Another reason older mills may not have expanded as rapidly as newer mills may be that older mills had already attained an optimal plant size and did not require additional spindle capacity during the decade under observation.

The remaining mill characteristics included in the regression models failed to show a statistically significant association with spindle growth in this analysis. Among the southern mills the estimate for KOL had the expected negative sign that would be consistent with the relatively lower wage-rental rate ratio found in this region. Also, the estimate for ROS was usually positive, which is consistent with the positive impact the ring spindle was thought to have on mill profitability. The absence of statistical significance in the case of ROS probably is due to the very high incidence of exclusive use of the ring spindle in the South, which led to little variability in the ROS variable in this period. The estimate for DPE had the anticipated positive sign, but the signs for the estimates for POP and FINE were inconsistent in the regressions for the southern mills.

In the North some regression estimates had the expected signs, but none was statistically significant. Both the adoption of the ring spindle and use of electricity were positively associated with spindle growth, as indicated by positive estimates of the coefficients of ROS and DPE. The signs of the remaining regression estimates were inconsistent as well as statistically insignificant, including estimates of the coefficients of KOL, POP, and FINE.

SUMMARY OF REGRESSION RESULTS

The analysis of the probability of mill survival to 1930 suggests that competitive strategies varied between regions. Successful mills in the South appear to have been among the newer mills and were located in smaller mill towns. Although adoption of the ring spindle likely was an important advantage for the region as a whole, too few southern mills used mule spindles by the twentieth century to find a statistical association between the type of spindle used and mill survival. In the North, however, enough mule spindles were still in use that the role of the ring spindle could be tested, and a link between the adoption of the ring spindle and mill survival was discovered. In addition, surviving northern mills tended to produce fine output, which is consistent with the theory that northern production shifted to higher grades of output because they could no longer compete with the southern branch of the industry in the markets for lower-grade output. Northern mills also apparently found an advantage to locating in relatively larger towns, which may have provided greater access to factor supplies and to agglomeration economies.

The second approach to the question of how mills succeeded in each region was to find mill strategies associated with faster mill spindle growth. Expansion of mill capacity was taken as a sign that a mill was financially healthy and had prospects for increased production and earnings in the future. In contrast to the first approach, the regressions for spindle growth found some similarities between the two regions. A larger mill size and shorter period of operation were associated with a higher-level spindle growth in both regions. Mill size was not associated with mill survival in the logit regressions in either region, but mill age appeared to hamper survival among southern mills as in the spindle growth regressions. The only parameter that seemed to find support in both approaches was mill age.

Although the two dependent variables, the odds of mill survival and spindle growth, are both measures of success in each region, perhaps it is not surprising that the same variables were not found to be correlated with each indicator. Mill survival divided mills into two extreme groups and did not distinguish among degrees of strength within those two categories. For example, among the group of mills that failed sometime before 1930, some were probably still financially healthy in 1900, the year of the first set of regressions. Mills may have been much less homogeneous within the two groups, survivors and non-survivors, than if the categories had been more narrowly defined. The second set of regressions was based on the continuous variable spindle growth, so mills could be differentiated more accurately using this indicator. Therefore different regression results would be expected.

The simple regression models presented here suggest that the mill directory data contain valuable information that helps distinguish surviving from failing mills, both on an interregional and intraregional basis. A number of extensions to this research are possible. Directories from the 1930s and 1940s could be investigated to track the continued decline of the northern mills. The period of textile depression in the 1920s could be studied in greater detail by examining the textile directories from each year of that decade, rather than at five-year intervals. Mills in other states could be added to the analysis to expand the coverage of the data in each region.

Alternative regression models might also be tested. Instead of considering only survival to 1930, the probability of surviving to various intervening years could be measured. A multiple-choice logit model could be used to estimate the odds of surviving to selected years (relative to survival to some other year).[4] The data permit estimation of the year of failure for each of the mills, based on their last appearance in the directories. By distinguishing among mills that failed relatively early from those that remained viable until the 1920s, mill survival would be defined more precisely. Since the relocation of the industry became most evident after 1920, when the South began to dominate total U.S. textile production, analysis of mills that failed in that decade would be most relevant to understanding the collapse of the northern industry.

The mill data could be pooled in a model that combines the cross-sectional and time-series data. So far only cross-sectional data have been analyzed by estimating regressions separately in different years. Changes in the relationships between mill survival and variables that might have influenced survival can be observed by comparing regression estimates from year to year. By pooling the data the impact of intertemporal changes in the independent variables (the mill characteristics) might be estimated more efficiently.

Alternative approaches to analyzing mill survival might be borrowed from the recent economic literature about savings and loans (S&L) institutions. Recent problems in the S&L industry have instigated a number of empirical studies of survival and failure of thrift institutions to aid federal regulations to better anticipate future failures. Some of the work on S&L failure is based on models using pooled data, but this approach is not without difficulties. The simplest version of the pooling approach is to classify S&Ls as either nonfailures or failures, where failed S&Ls are treated as nonfailures up to the period they failed. One problem with this method is that it probably weights nonfailures heavily, since failed S&Ls drop out of the data after their last period and contribute to the nonfailure observations before that (Maddala 1986, 18). As a result the pooled sample of, say, ninety-nine surviving S&Ls and one failure over a ten-year period will contain 999 non-failure observations and one failure (if that S&L failed in the last period). The pooled sample weights failure by 1-in-1,000 observations, whereas the failure rate was actually 1-in-100. Another deficiency of this approach is that the shift from financial health to failure is abrupt in the model. To capture the transition between the two conditions, "time-to-failure," Markovian, and other dynamic models might be used, but the data from the textile directories are probably too limited to permit more sophisticated analyses of this sort (Maddala 1986).

NOTES

1. Models of qualitative choice include linear probability, probit, and logit models (see R. S. Pindyck and D. L. Rubinfeld 1976, Chapter 8).

2. This approach is suggested by E. E. Leamer (1983).

3. Cathy McHugh (1981) notes that the education and health services provided in the mill village served to create a more productive labor force. Also, the provision of living quarters helped to recruit mature workers, by offering housing for workers with families.

4. For a description of multiple-choice models, see Pindyck and Rubinfeld (1976, Chapter 8).

7

Evaluation of the Theories about the Relocation

SUPPORT FOR TECHNOLOGICAL CHANGE HYPOTHESIS

The adoption of the ring spindle was examined in the previous chapters to find what role technological innovation played in the growth of the cotton textile industry in the period 1880 to 1930. Textile directories listed the number of ring and mule spindles in the mills each year, and the share of ring spindles in total mill spindles was calculated for each mill reporting the composition of spindle equipment. The ring-spindle ratio indicates to what extent mills converted to the newer ring model after 1880 and is one measure of the rate of innovation in the textile industry in this period.

The descriptive analysis of the directory data presented in Chapter 3 showed that the southern mills used the ring spindle almost exclusively from early in the period. Only a handful of southern mills in the sample used mule spindles. The northern mills had a significantly lower average ring-spindle ratio compared with the southern mills each year. The northern ring-spindle ratio rose steadily throughout the period, however, which indicates that the northern mills were adopting the new technology as well.

The technological change hypothesis is that the pace of the textile relocation was controlled by the rate of improvements in textile machinery. Hekman (1980) has suggested that the gradual takeover of the U.S. textile industry by the southern mills in this period was linked to the introduction of skilled-labor-saving technological changes. The new machinery allowed the southern industry to use inexperienced workers when the mills were first introduced to the region, Hekman argues. As the models were modified to produce higher grades of output, the southern mills expanded their range of products and eventually dominated the national textile markets.

The technological change hypothesis was tested by observing the association between the adoption of the ring spindle and mill survival in each region. If the new technology facilitated the expansion of the southern industry, one would expect that the successful mills in the South would have used those machines to a greater extent than mills that failed. Successful northern mills would also be expected to have favored the new models of textile machinery, if the new technology was more profitable than the older models.[1]

The analysis of mill survival presented in Chapter 5 indicated that surviving southern mills had somewhat higher ring-spindle ratios each year than nonsurviving mills in the region, although the ratio was high in both groups. In the North the surviving mills had noticeably higher ring-spindle ratios in the earlier part of the period compared with nonsurviving northern mills. In the early twentieth century the decision to adopt the ring spindle apparently had an effect on a mill's fate in that region. The ring-spindle ratio was nearly equal in both groups of northern mills after 1910, though. It appears that by the time the southern mills had begun to dominate the industry, it may have been too late for northern mills to overcome the disadvantages the northern branch of the industry faced. In spite of the effort to modernize the northern mills could not remain competitive with the South, most likely because of unfavorably high wages in the North.

In the analysis of survival among mills in the same city, adoption of the ring spindle appeared to have been an important factor. Although the ring was used almost exclusively among the southern mills included in Table 5.3, ring use in the North generally differentiated the surviving from the failing mills. For the bulk of the northern mills and cities represented in that

analysis, the average ring-spindle ratio was higher among surviving mills than nonsurviving.

The association between survival and the adoption of the ring
is analyzed more precisely by the logit regression of the probability of mill survival that was presented in Chapter 6. The
regressions of the odds of mill survival and several mill characteristics were estimated for mills operating in 1900, separated
by state. The northern mills revealed a positive association between survival to 1930 and reliance on the ring spindle. The
southern mills included in the regression used only ring spindles, which prevented a test of the hypothesis because there
was no variation in the ring-share variable. Other factors were
associated with mill survival in each region, however, including the population of the mill town, the grade of output produced, and the age of the mill. A mill's age may also have been
related to spindle choice, if new mills favored the ring spindle
and old mills were ready scrap their spindle stock in favor of
the ring spindle. The logit regression results suggest that, while
the spindle choice may not have been the only determining
factor in mill survival, the decision to adopt the ring spindle
was certainly associated with survival in the North.

LABOR

Alternative hypotheses about the pace of the relocation of
the textile industry focus on the role of labor and capital as
constraints to the development of the industry in the South, as
discussed in Chapter 2. The labor hypothesis holds that growth
of the southern textile industry was limited by the development of skills and experience among the southern textile labor
force. The directory listings did not provide much information
for evaluating the role of labor in the growth of the industry in
each region, however. Only total employment figures were
provided, without any further labor classifications. The employment data were essentially a measure of mill size, and the
labor, capital, and total spindles numbers were highly correlated. The limited employment data were useful in calculating
the capital-labor ratio of each mill but did not help assess the
role of labor skills in hindering the southern mills.

Population data available from the directories provided a test for the importance of locating near a pool of labor, to the extent mill labor was supplied by the local population. The analysis of mill survival in Chapters 5 and 6 indicated that the surviving northern mills were located in larger mill towns than the non-surviving mills, but that the opposite was true in the South. This result is consistent with the dependence in the North on immigrant workers, who were more likely to have lived in the larger northern cities. The population of mill towns in the South may not have mattered to mill survival because of the relatively small size of southern towns due to low population density in that rural region.

Although location appears to have influenced northern mill survival, the role of labor skills and experience in each region remains uncertain because of deficiencies in the data. Oates has suggested, however, that mill location probably was determined by factors other than proximity to a pool of experienced textile labor, including the proximity to capital, transportation centers, and power resources (1981, 72).

Despite the limitations in the labor statistics provided by the textile directories, the labor hypothesis can be evaluated in light of the literature on the textile industry. Historians have made two compelling arguments that reduce the importance of labor experience in the growth of the southern textile industry: textile production had few skill requirements, and there was little difference in the quality of northern and southern textile labor.

Although the southern mill workers undoubtedly gained experience as the textile industry matured in the South in this period, as Wright (1981) has argued, it is unlikely that inexperience constrained the development of the industry in that region. Most textile jobs had few skill requirements, and mill labor could be trained adequately in little time (Galenson 1975, 147). In his visit to the southern mills, Uttley was "told that probably not 10 per cent of the hands had been in a factory before, but this does not seem to be a serious drawback, as they are quick to learn" (1905, 44). Even if southern textile workers were less experienced and skilled than northern textile workers, the introduction of the ring spindle and the automatic loom reduced the skills required in textile production.

Southern mill labor may not have been any less experienced than northern labor, however. Northern mills relied heavily on immigrants, who had little previous industrial experience when they first entered the mills. The majority of northern immigrants were farmers prior to employment in the mills (Lahne 1944, 5). Thus there was little difference between the training required of northern and southern mill workers when they joined the payroll.

Moreover, there were numerous accounts of the adequacy of southern labor. Mitchell reported that northern superintendents in southern mills were satisfied with the southern labor force, and he quotes contemporary southern observers who remarked that the quality of southern workers was as high as in the North (1921, 171). The president of one southern mill said at the time that "There is no more trouble teaching [southern workers] than at any other point. In fact, it is far better than the average help in New England, which is now mostly foreign emigrants . . . it takes no longer here than anywhere else" (Uttley 1905, 59).

Lack of experience among southern mill workers in the early period of mill construction in the South may not have hindered the progress of the industry in that region, according to these accounts. Mill workers were quickly trained, especially following the introduction of skilled-labor-saving innovations. In addition, northern mill workers, who were predominantly foreign immigrants, were no more experienced than workers in the South in this period, which equalized the quality of mill labor between the two regions.

CAPITAL

The hypothesis that the underdeveloped southern capital market hindered the textile industry relocation remains controversial. As noted in Chapter 2, the interest-rate differentials that persisted between the North and the South in this period are consistent with a variety of explanations. The differentials may have reflected information costs and higher risk involved in lending to southern borrowers, which could have existed even in perfect capital markets. Capital market imperfections would have introduced market power on the part of financial inter-mediaries, and higher interest rates in the South would have been set by local monopolists in that regional capital market. The differentials might reflect some combination of these two factors, for example, if southern banks enjoyed monopoly rents but were also compensated for the higher risks of lending to newly established southern mills.

The risk of lending to the southern mills is well documented in the directory data. The survival rate of mills in North Caro-lina, shown in Table 3.6, reveals a high rate of failure in this period. Moreover, the failure rate steadily declined over time, which is consistent with the narrowing of the interest-rate dif-ferentials between the South and other regions later in the pe-riod.[2] The southern survival rate was lower than in the North at first, as indicated by the survival rates of Massachusetts mills that are also shown in Table 3.6. Twenty-three percent of northern mills in existence in 1885 survived to 1930, whereas only 16 percent of the southern mills became survivors. Unfor-tunately, the directories do not provide information for evalu-ating the other explanations for the existence of the interest-rate differentials of this period.

Another point of debate is whether the capital available to the southern mills constrained the growth of mills in that re-gion. The South had access to capital from other than financial institutions, because northern capital migrated via direct in-vestment, and northern machine companies and commission houses extended credit to the southern mills. In addition, the southern mills apparently had access to local capital, judging by the high rate of southern ownership of the capital stock of southern mills. The evidence that the southern mills relied pri-marily on local sources of capital does not address the issue of the adequacy of southern capital, however. In fact, because northern capital contributed a minor part of the southern mill capital stock, the development of southern financial systems would probably have boosted the growth of southern capital by facilitating the migration of capital from the North.

The directory data on mill capital stocks shown in Table 5.2 suggest that larger and better-capitalized mills were more likely to survive in both regions. Surviving mills in the North and in the South had higher average capital stocks each year than nonsurviving mills in those regions. Also, the northern mills were significantly larger than the southern mills, which is consistent with both the greater availability of capital in the North and the riskier nature of the newer southern mills. Capital market constraints may have contributed to the relatively small scale of southern mills compared with northern mills.

This link between capital and survival was not supported in other tests presented in this study, however, which failed to find a direct association between capital levels and mill survival. The analysis of survival within cities did not reveal higher capital values in larger cities, nor was survival distinguished by the level of mill capital (see Table 5.3). Rather, surviving and nonsurviving mills tended to show similar levels of capital on a city-by-city basis, which suggests that mill scale was determined by local factor prices. Regression analysis in Chapter 6 also failed to discover a statistically significant correlation between mill survival (or growth in spindle capacity) and the level of mill capital.

The importance of access to capital is suggested indirectly by the association, found in the logit regressions discussed in Chapter 6, between mill survival in the North and a larger mill-town population. Town size may have indicated proximity to financial centers in the North, which were likely to be located in the more populous areas. The absence of that association in the South may be explained by the lack of any financial centers in North Carolina, due to the dispersion of the region's population at that time.

The mill data in this study provide some casual support for the view that regional capital availability may have determined mill size and location, based on some evidence that the level of capital and population of the mill town contributed to mill survival. The findings were not consistently supported in the variety of tests presented in the study, however. Further research is required to sort out the differences between the statistical descriptions of the mills in Chapters 3 through 5 and the regressions based on the same directory data in Chapter 6. Moreover, limitations in the directory data, which do not provide specific information about the regional capital markets (besides the level of each mill's capital stock), leave the larger issue of southern capital market imperfections and the pace of the industry relocation unresolved.

NOTES

1. Adoption of the ring may have been slowed in the North by previous investment in mule spindles in that region, however. In the early twentieth century the capital-cost savings by postponing a switch to the ring spindle and continuing to use installed mule spindles may have been a profit-maximizing strategy (Feller 1966, 1968).

2. The relative weakness of the northern industry became apparent early, however, judging by the higher rate of survival among mills in the South than in the North from 1900 through the 1920s (see Table 5.3). But because the textile industry was just one among many sectors in the northern economy, the higher risk implied by less favorable survival rates relative to the South probably would not have influenced the interest-rate differential.

8

Textile Wage Differentials and Equalization

REGIONAL TEXTILE WAGE DIFFERENTIALS

Lower textile wages were the primary advantage that southern mills had in competition with the North. Wage differentials between the two regions are well documented. Wage data collected by the Bureau of Labor Statistics show that northern textile wages were sometimes as much as twice the level of southern wages in the late nineteenth century.[1] For one example of the regional wage differentials in this period, the relationship between average textile wages in North Carolina and Massachusetts is reported in Table 8.1. The ratio of textile wages in North Carolina to wages in Massachusetts, both representative textile states, fluctuated between 43 and 90 percent in the period 1878 to 1928. A wage gap of the same magnitude was found by Richard Lester in similar calculations that included wage statistics from the four primary textile producing states in each region between 1890 and 1940 (1945, 339). Galenson offers ample evidence of a regional wage differential for various categories of mill occupations based on census of manufactures data (1975, 166).

Lower wages would have been an important advantage in textile production because labor costs constituted a large share of total production costs. The U.S. Commissioner of Labor reported in 1891 that labor costs in northern mills were about 35

Table 8.1
Ratio of North Carolina to Massachusetts Textile Wages

Year	Ratio	Year	Ratio
1878	.434	1909	.733
1881	.446	1910	.722
1882	.474	1911	.751
1884	.485	1912	.722
1885	.589	1913	.735
1888	.546	1914	.761
1889	.558	1916	.669
1890	.567	1918	.699
1894	.592	1920	.896
1895	.565	1922	.711
1899	.619	1924	.676
1900	.534	1926	.698
1907	.647	1928	.769
1908	.661		

Source: U.S. Bureau of Labor Statistics, Bulletin #604
Note: Based on a simple average of the average hourly earnings for loom-fixers, male weavers, female weavers, and female frame spinners.

percent of the total costs of producing print cloth and were exceeded only by materials costs, which formed about 55 percent of total costs (Smith 1944, 67). Copeland estimates that labor costs ranged from 7 to 45 percent of total production costs, increasing with the fineness of cloth produced (1912, 250).

A number of explanations for the observed regional wage gap have been offered. Lower southern wages have been attributed to lower productivity, a lower regional cost of living, fewer manufacturing alternatives in the South, developments in the farm sector, and various labor-market imperfections. Following a review of these arguments, the pattern of changes in the regional wage ratio will be examined. The tendency for regional textile wages to converge by the 1920s is of particular interest. Next, a new approach to analyzing the regional textile wage gap is taken by considering the international trade literature on factor price differentials and the process of factor price equalization.

Some textile industry historians argue that southern wages

were lower than northern because of lower productivity among southern workers. As a result, southern mills may not have enjoyed lower labor costs per unit of output if lower wages were offset by lower productivity. Southern textile workers generally came to the mills from the farms and were inexperienced with manufacturing work. Wright (1981) notes the gap in labor skills between mill workers in the North and the South and emphasizes the role of labor experience accumulation in the progress of the industry in the South, as was discussed in Chapter 2. In addition, southern workers were often criticized as undisciplined and unreliable. Southern mills commonly maintained about a 25 percent surplus labor force of "spare help" to accommodate the frequent absenteeism among southern mill workers (Kohn 1907, 61). Part of the attendance problem was due to workers leaving the mills to help plant and harvest crops back on their family farms. By contrast, northern workers apparently worked continuously, and northern mills reported no problem with absenteeism in that region.

Measures of regional labor productivity reveal that southern mill labor was less productive than northern, but not by enough to explain the entire wage gap between the two regions. Galenson (1975) estimated the ratio of output per worker between the South and the North, adjusted for cost of materials and the longer hours worked in the southern mills, between 1879 and 1919. Southern productivity fluctuated between 60 and 77 percent of northern productivity between 1879 and 1909 and then rose to between 83 and 91 percent by 1919 (1975, 169). Still, the productivity gap remained far smaller than the wage gap in that period. This suggests that lower wages more than offset any productivity handicap of southern workers relative to northern.

The productivity gap calculated by Galenson declined after 1910, which she attributed to a rise in the southern capital-labor ratio relative to that in the North (1975, 170). One measure of the capital-labor ratio, the number of active spindles per wage earner, clearly rose faster in the South than in the North, especially after 1900 (1975, 171). Other factors that may have contributed to productivity growth in the South include the use of more efficient machinery and accumulation of labor skills over time. Prior to 1900 southern mills commonly operated second-hand machinery that was purchased from the northern mills. Later, southern machinery was newer and more modern than northern, which likely contributed to improvements in labor productivity in that period. Although Wright's hypothesis that the southern labor force experienced "learning-by-doing" is difficult to document, he presents evidence that suggests that the composition of the mill labor force matured over time and probably became more productive as well (see Chapter 2). In any event, productivity improvements fail to fully account for the observed regional wage differentials.

Others point to regional differences in the cost of living that might have resulted in equal real wages between regions, even though nominal wages did not equalize. The southern cost of living may have been lower than the northern, which could account for lower nominal wages in the South. Southern housing and fuel costs were commonly subsidized by the mills, and southern families that lived in mill towns received various services that constituted non-wage compensation. By several accounts, the rent in southern mill villages ranged from one-third to one-half of that in northern mill cities throughout the period of competition between the two regions (Chen 1941, 543). Wood and coal for home heating were supplied by southern mills at favorable prices, and water and electricity were also provided at a discount (Chen 1941, 542; Backman and Gainsbrugh 1946, 89). Mills operated company stores, where goods were sold at below-market levels, probably because mill stores bought provisions in large volumes at a discount (Chen 1941, 544). Schools, health facilities, and community recreation centers were often provided by mill villages, especially those located in remote areas (Berglund, Starnes, and Traver de Vyver 1930, 120).

Although historians agree that southern mill villages offered these advantages, the conclusion that the southern cost of living was lower than in the North remains controversial. Northern mill labor also enjoyed many of the public services that were offered in the South, but those northern services were financed by the mills indirectly, through local taxes (Lahne 1944, 168). Thus, non-wage compensation in the North may have been near that in the South and would not account for the regional wage gap.

Estimates of regional cost-of-living indices fail to show a consistent difference between the North and the South in this period. Don Bellante (1979) points out that we do not have reliable historical price data for calculating real-wage differentials that may have existed in the past. Various historical cost-of-living comparisons have been made, but the methodology of the studies varied widely, as did the results. The National Industrial Conference Board studied the cost of living of cotton mill employees in the two regions in 1920 and found that costs were actually higher in two of the larger southern mill towns, Greenville, South Carolina, and Charlotte, North Carolina, than in Lawrence and Fall River, Massachusetts (Mitchell and Mitchell 1930, 15). Other studies have found no significant difference between prices in the two regions in the 1920s (Berglund et al. 1930, 128–51; Bernstein 1960, 9). Moreover, the impact of non-wage compensation provided by southern mill villages on southern wages remains uncertain. Southern wages did not appear to vary depending on whether the worker lived in a mill village or on the extent of services provided by a mill (Berglund et al. 1930, 154; Lemert 1933, 135).

Even if southern workers are assumed to have enjoyed a lower cost of living through non-wage compensation provided by southern mills, this advantage still fails to account for much of the regional difference in textile wages. Chen Han Chen adjusted the nominal textile wages for the average level of expenditures made by workers in each region in 1889 to estimate a real-wage index that would account for a lower cost of living in the South. He found that real wages remained 20 to 30 percent higher in the North than in the South, compared with about a 40 percent differential based on nominal wages (1941, 544–45).

Various conditions in the labor markets in each region may have contributed to interregional wage differentials in this period. Galenson (1975) has argued that differences in the elasticity of the supply curve of labor led to higher wages in the North than in the South. Supply elasticity, which measures the responsiveness of the quantity of labor supplied to changes in the wage rate, was lower in the South, where workers had fewer types of alternative employment to compare with employment opportunities in the mills. As a result, a relatively small rise in wages was sufficient to induce more labor to enter the mills. There were several types of manufacturing industries that competed for labor in the North, however, which led to a steeper, or less elastic, supply curve for labor in that region. As a result,

> The most likely explanation of the rapid increase in textile employment in the South, coupled with small or negative wage increases, is that the southern industry was expanding along a very elastic supply curve of labor. The northern experience of smaller employment increases and higher wage increases is consistent with a less elastic supply curve of labor in that region than in the South. (Galenson 1975, 164–65)

The main problem with this argument is that southern wages actually rose faster than northern to close the interregional wage gap between 1880 and 1930. A lower elasticity of the supply of labor in the South might explain the initial low level of southern wages but is not consistent with the pattern of southern wage convergence toward northern levels later in the period.

The primary alternative employment for mill labor in the South was farming, and changes in commodity prices and farm wages likely affected the southern textile wage. A large proportion of the southern labor force was employed in agriculture before 1930; the share was as high as 90 percent in 1880. Fluctuations in the price of cotton affected the flow of labor between agriculture and textile production. Low cotton prices induced some farmers to seek mill employment, and high cotton prices created labor shortages for the mills.

For example, the depression in cotton that began in 1893 caused an "exodus from the farm" that provided labor for the cotton mills that were rapidly being built, and when cotton prices recovered after 1900, labor began to return to the farms (Copeland 1912, 40). Contemporary observers reported a shortage of labor in the mills when cotton prices recovered. "At the time of my visit to the South there was a scarcity of labour for the mills of South Carolina and Georgia, partly owing . . . to the fact that the high price of cotton was attracting the hands back to the farms again" (Uttley 1905, 44–45). By the 1920s depressed cotton prices, the boll weevil problem, and urbanization of the southern population contributed to a return of labor from farming to the manufacturing sector (Mitchell and Mitchell 1930, 140). Hence, relatively low southern textile wages might reflect periods of low cotton prices, according to this argument. While farm wages probably had some influence on textile wages, other factors that take into account the demand for textile labor and changes in southern labor productivity seem to be more consistent with the observed changes in the interregional wage differential than do conditions in the farming sector, however.

The presence of labor unions is another possible explanation that has been investigated by several authors for relatively high wages in the North. There is general agreement that union power was never strong enough to account for interregional wage differentials in this period, however. Only a small percentage of textile labor was affiliated with one of the several textile unions before 1930, and organized strikes had an insignificant impact on textile wages or work load in that period (Galenson 1975, 130–44). Striking workers reportedly were easily replaced by non-union labor in either region. Uttley noted that a northern fine-good mill that had trouble with employees "had solved the difficulty by putting non-union men in their places, not the only instance I had met with which seemed to show that, though the hands are organized, there is often enough non-union help to take their places in case of a strike in a small department of a mill" (1905, 28). In the South a high rate of labor mobility within the region and influx of labor from the farms during periods of cotton depressions weakened the ability of striking workers to protect their jobs, which in turn discourages that activity (Mitchell and Mitchell 1930, 139–40).

Unions had a stronger presence in the North than in the South, owing to the long history of organization among mule spinners, the highest paid and most skilled among textile workers. The mule spinners' union was eventually weakened by growth in the use of ring spindles and the influx of immigrants in the North in the late nineteenth century, who were resistant to organization (Copeland 1912, 124). Southern textile workers remained essentially unorganized until the 1930s, in spite of six separate strike incidents in the South that were staged by northern unions in the late 1920s (Bernstein 1960, 40). Strong public sentiment against unions, due to the individualistic character of the southern people, plus the geographic scattering of southern mills discouraged the union movement in the South (Copeland 1912, 128). Irving Bernstein also points out that the strike activity in the 1920s occurred during a period of depression in the industry, when excess labor supply and excess capacity rendered employers unreceptive to wage demands (1960, 41).

Low southern textile wages tended to catch up to the northern wage level over the period of industry relocation. The ratio of southern to northern wages increased (unevenly) between 1880 and 1930, as shown in Table 8.1. More rapid growth in textile production in the South most likely explains the general gains in southern wages relative to the North. For example, the 30 percent rise in average textile wages between 1902 and 1907 in South Carolina led one observer to remark that "Of course the demand for labor and the prosperity of the mills have been responsible for this increase" (Kohn 1907, 32). Mitchell later noted that growth of the industry in the South gave "wages an upward trend that, despite lapses and spurts, has been strong and inevitable; wages have advanced not gradually, but in jumps mainly as a consequence of accelerated mill building" (1921, 229).

Several events had an impact on the interregional wage ratio that led to irregularities in the pattern of wage convergence in this period. Restrictions on foreign immigration to the United States that were imposed after 1914 sharply reduced the growth of labor supply for northern mills and probably put pressure on northern textile wages relative to southern in the late–1910s. Immigrant labor was an important part of the northern mill labor force, as high as about 70 percent by 1910, whereas southern mill workers were almost entirely native to that region. Rising northern textile wages in response to curtailed immigration may explain the widening of interregional wage differentials between 1914 and 1920. The wage gap then closed with the arrival of war, which boosted labor demand in both regions. Subsequent improvements in southern wages relative to northern in the 1920s were probably due more to weakness in northern wages, as that sector began to decline, rather than to growth in southern wages. Estimates of southern textile wages in the 1920s, after adjusting for price effects, show a fairly steady level pattern up to 1930 (Wright 1981, 622).[2]

The strength of textile wages in the South in spite of depressed conditions in the industry during the 1920s has a number of possible explanations. As mentioned in Chapter 3, Wright (1981) suggests that higher southern real wages in the 1920s (after adjusting for changes in the price level) were the result of disequilibrium in the labor market. Real wages were higher in the 1920s compared with prior years because nominal (money) wages failed to decline with the disinflation following the war. In his scenario, textile workers actively resisted wage cuts that would have been necessary to reach an equilibrium in the labor market, and excess labor supply resulted. Wright's evidence that labor successfully kept nominal wages at above market-clearing levels is not persuasive, however. As noted above, textile strikes were particularly ineffective in either region during this period, and union power was weak in the textile industry before 1930.

Although Wright dismisses other explanations for the pattern of real wages in the South before 1930, these alternatives seem more promising than his market failure approach. Strength in real wages might reflect the gains in labor productivity that were achieved in the South after 1900 because of a rising capital-labor ratio in the southern textile industry (Galenson 1975, 170). This could account for the fact that southern farm wages remained fairly flat after 1900, while textile wages jumped during the war and stayed at a new, higher level afterwards. Moreover, population migration flows are consistent with the strengthening in textile wages in the 1920s. The significant increase in out-migration of southern whites between 1920 and 1930 would have reduced the supply of textile labor and supported textile wages in that period. Wright has downplayed the role of white out-migration by arguing that the bulk of out-migration was accounted for by black labor, and the textile in-

Table 8.2
Population Migration, by Region
(Thousands)

South[a]

Decade	Net Migration	per 1,000[c]	Native White	Foreign	Negro
1870-80	-89	-20	-45	4	-49
1880-90	-125	-27	-85	11	-51
1890-1900	-261	-49	-125	7	-143
1900-10	-251	-41	-129	17	-139
1910-20	-367	-49	-128	10	-249
1920-30	-829	-102	-272	4	-561

North[b]

Decade	Net Migration	per 1,000[c]	Native White	Foreign	Negro
1870-80	145	50	-36	177	4
1880-90	343	88	-14	351	6
1890-1900	405	87	27	366	12
1900-10	387	72	-52	433	7
1910-20	193	16	-52	237	8
1920-30	-16	-14	-171	153	2

Source: Population Census
[a] Northern states: Maine, Massachusetts, New Hampshire, Rhode Island
[b] Southern states: Alabama, Georgia, North Carolina, South Carolina
[c] Net migration per 1,000 of the average population between census years

dustry employed primarily white labor. Nevertheless, the evidence of population flows, shown in Table 8.2, reveals that white-labor out-migration was large enough to have had an impact on that segment of the southern labor market.

Although several of the above-mentioned explanations likely played a role in determining the level and changes in regional textile wages, this discussion can also be attacked from the viewpoint of the international trade literature. Trade models are applicable to studies of regions as well as nations, since many of the characteristics of international comparisons hold for interregional comparisons, with the exception that regions are not separated by political boundaries.

FACTOR PRICE EQUALIZATION

The process of the equalization of U.S. regional textile wages can be analyzed from the viewpoint of the international trade literature. International economics models predict that international or interregional wages may equalize, even if labor is not mobile between countries or regions. Specifically, the factor price equalization theorem (FPE) implies that, under strict conditions, the wages and rental rates in two regions will be equal through the transfer of either goods or factors.

When factors can move between regions (countries), factor prices will equalize because factor flows will tend to eliminate any factor price differentials. For example, if wages are higher in one region, high wages will attract new supplies of labor from the low-wage region. The increased labor supply will reduce wages in the high-wage region and raise wages in the low-wage region. Labor flows will continue until wages are equalized.[3] Even when factors are immobile, however, factor prices may equalize, if the conditions for FPE hold. The important contribution of FPE is that trade in commodities can substitute for factor migration and achieve equalization of factor prices.

FPE in a two-region, two-factor, two-commodity model requires perfectly competitive factor and product markets, identical production functions for each commodity between regions, linear homogeneous production functions,[4] nonreversible and different factor intensities of the two commodities at all factor prices, incomplete specialization, homogeneous factors, and absence of trade barriers and transportation costs (Samuelson 1948).

Trade in commodities works to equalize factor prices because of the link between product prices and factor earnings under the assumptions that have been laid out. Product prices will equalize under free trade, since consumers in both countries will purchase a good where it is cheapest. If a product price is lower in one location, demand will drive up that price until prices are equal in all locations. Since perfect competition implies that product prices equal the marginal cost of producing the commodity, equality of product prices means that marginal costs will be equal in both regions. Because factor earnings are a function of product cost, and production functions are the same in both areas, factor prices will equalize.

Although some of the strict assumptions that are required for FPE may be relaxed, the theory might be criticized for its limited applicability to real-world conditions. FPE can be generalized to any number of countries, as long as the remaining assumptions are fulfilled, and to any number of commodities and factors, as long as the number of commodities is equal to or greater than the number of factors. The remaining conditions are necessary for FPE, however, primarily because the link between product prices, marginal cost, and factor earnings is broken if any of the other restrictions are relaxed. The theory may still be useful even though the world does not conform to these strict conditions, however. Some authors predict that factor prices will tend to equalize as the theoretical conditions for FPE become more closely approximated (Chacholiades 1978, 283). In fact, the power of the theory is supported by evidence discussed later that wages appear to be equalizing worldwide, which may be interpreted as a trend leading toward FPE (Magee 1980, 58).

The historical evidence is consistent with a tendency toward equalization of factor prices between the North and South in the period 1880 to 1930, although equalization was not complete. The wage gap between the two regions narrowed, as indicated by the textile wage differential that was reported in Table 8.1 (but southern wages remained below northern at the end of the period). Capital rental rates also tended to equalize in this period, based on estimates of regional interest rates. Interest-rate equalization can imply rental-rate equalization if depreciation rates and the price of the capital good are assumed equal in both regions, and if there is positive gross capital formation in each region (Samuelson 1965).[5] Davis (1965) found that U.S. interregional interest differentials existed in the late nineteenth century but were reduced over the period 1869–1914. Interest-rate differentials between the South and other regions tended to narrow at that time, but at a slower pace than in the rest of the nation.

Since travel was relatively expensive during this period, and capital markets were still underdeveloped, it is reasonable to assume that capital and labor were immobile in the late nineteenth century. In this type of environment, the FPE theorem predicts that interregional trade in commodities would substitute for factor migration and lead to equalization in wages and rental rates, assuming all other conditions hold. In other words, market imperfections, use of different production functions, specialization in one of the commodities, differences in the characteristics of the factors, or tariffs imply that the theory would no longer predict FPE (although it may still occur).

In addition to asking why FPE failed in this period, the issue of what drove the trend toward FPE should be examined. Conditions likely changed over the period of the relocation of the textile industry that led to better satisfaction of the requirements for FPE. One important development was industrialization of the South, which altered the composition of southern output. Because of the South's endowment of arable land, southern production was almost completely specialized in agriculture in the late nineteenth century. As noted earlier, complete specialization would have violated one of the conditions for FPE and probably explains, in large part, the wide differences in factor prices between the South and the rest of the United States in the late nineteenth century. The gradual shift to manufacturing production in the South between 1880 and 1930 meant that southern output became less specialized over this period, and the incomplete specialization requirement for FPE would have been satisfied. The composition of regional output is reported in Table 8.3, based on the values of agricultural and manufacturing production in the South from 1880 to 1930. The share of southern output made up of agricultural products declined from 88 percent in 1880 to only 30 percent by 1930, reflecting the dramatic process of industrialization within the region in this period.

Besides complete specialization, transportation costs also vi-

Table 8.3
Regional Output Composition, 1880–1930
(Percentage of Total Regional Output)

Year	South		North	
	Agriculture	Manufacturing	Agriculture	Manufacturing
1880	88.0%	12.0%	9.0%	91.0%
1890	74.0	26.0	6.3	93.7
1900	68.1	31.9	8.0	92.0
1910	60.6	39.4	6.8	93.2
1920	56.4	43.6	4.8	95.2
1930	30.2	69.8	4.7	95.3

Source: Census of Agriculture, Census of Manufactures

olated a condition for FPE. Transportation costs would have introduced a wedge between the foreign and domestic prices of a commodity, which would have prevented the equalization of product prices and, hence, factor prices. The development of various modes of transportation and communication in this period reduced transportation costs markedly, however, and may have contributed to the observed trend toward FPE, as product prices neared equality between the South and the rest of the United States.

Another source of problems for the FPE model in this period stems from imperfections in the capital markets in the late nineteenth century, as was discussed in Chapter 2. Monopoly power may have been enjoyed by banks in the underdeveloped capital markets of the late nineteenth century, which would have prevented equalization of interest rates and capital rental rates through trade, as predicted by the FPE theory. Hence the evolution of a national capital market would have contributed to FPE by creating a more competitive factor market. Of course, a national capital market also promoted equalization of capital factor prices directly by facilitating interregional capital mobility.

Most of the remaining requirements for FPE were likely to

have been satisfied in this period. Aside from capital markets, the remaining product and factor markets were competitive. The cotton textile market was well integrated at the national level, and cotton products were thought to be standardized and competitively priced (Backman and Gainsbrugh 1946, 124, 142, 168). Labor mobility was high within each region and labor markets were competitive in both the North and the South, because workers had alternative opportunities among the various manufacturing industries in the North and in agriculture in the South. In addition, unionism had little impact in the North and was virtually nonexistent in the South at this time.

Production functions were probably identical in both regions, although we lack empirical estimates of regional production functions. Based on the experience of the textile industry, the flow of technology and information was apparently unhindered, judging by the number of articles published in national journals such as *Textile World*. Textile producers in each region undoubtedly had the same production functions available to them. Mills chose different production techniques, however, as evidenced by the use of different machinery and levels of capital intensity in each region.[6] Other features of textile production, for example, returns to scale or presence of factor intensity reversals remain potential problems, however.

INTERNATIONAL WAGE EQUALIZATION

International wages appear to be catching up to the traditionally high U.S. average manufacturing wage, which can be interpreted as evidence consistent with the FPE theory (Magee 1980, 58). Calculations of foreign wages relative to U.S. wages show that the gap has been narrowing. The average manufacturing wage in various countries relative to the U.S. average manufacturing wage is reported in the first column of Table 8.4, based on 1970 data. The evidence shows that the less-developed countries tended to report lower average wages relative to the United States, not surprisingly. The rate of growth of wages between 1970 and 1980 in the low-wage countries was faster than in high-wage countries, however. Wage growth relative to the growth in U.S. wages during the 1970s is reported

Table 8.4
International Wage Convergence to U.S. Wage, 1970–1980

Country	Relative Wage 1970	Relative Wage Growth 1970-1980
Korea	8	188
Turkey	9	89
Singapore	11	45
Cyprus	15	93
Greece	16	131
Yugoslavia	16	56
Mexico	26	8
Finland	35	106
France	35	111
Japan	38	134
United Kingdom	38	71
Austria	40	115
Belgium	40	163
Norway	42	67
New Zealand	43	51
Switzerland	44	168
Australia	50	70
Germany	53	85
South Africa	78	17
Sweden	85	51
Canada	89	3

Source: Yearbook of Labor Statistics, International Labor Office, 1980.

in the second column of Table 8.4. Generally, the lower a country's wage relative to the United States in 1970, the faster the wage growth in the following decade.

Part of the change in relative wages can be explained by exchange-rate fluctuations. For example, when the U.S. dollar depreciates against another currency, the dollar value of foreign wages would rise and the international wage gap would narrow. Estimates of real-wage differentials, which account for exchange-rate changes, reveal a similar pattern of equalization, however.

Daniel J. B. Mitchell (1983) presents evidence of convergence of foreign wages to U.S. levels during the period 1960–1980 for nine developed countries. He computes two series of foreign wages relative to U.S. wages, nominal and real. The first series converts foreign wages to dollars at the prevailing exchange rate to obtain a nominal relative wage series, and the second deflates foreign wages using the foreign inflation index and then converts to dollars at the base year exchange rate.

Mitchell finds a consistent narrowing of the foreign wage gap relative to U.S. wages, although the convergence of real wages is less complete than for nominal wages. For example, nominal wages in Japan rose from 10 percent of U.S. wages in 1960 to 56 percent in 1980 and the real wage index rose from 10 percent in 1960 to 24 percent in 1980. During this period the U.S. dollar depreciated sharply and accounted for much of the convergence in Japanese nominal wages relative to the United States. Similar results were found for Belgium, France, West Germany, Italy, Netherlands, Sweden, and the United Kingdom, where the depreciation of the dollar yielded real relative wages that were about half the nominal wage ratio of each country. Nevertheless, a definite trend toward wage equalization is apparent, even after accounting for exchange-rate trends.

After documenting international wage convergence to U.S. levels, Mitchell investigates the forces behind the wage equalization process. He tests two potential explanations, the first based on trade flows and the FPE theory, and the second on changes in factor supplies and development theory. The model for FPE, explained earlier, is based on a one-period analysis of the impact of trade and product price equalization on factor earnings, where factor supplies are immobile and in fixed supply (in the immediate period). The alternative theory allows variability in factor supplies, which would influence factor prices by altering the marginal productivity of the factor and possibly changing the relative capital-labor ratio within each country. Factor supplies may rise through population growth or increased saving and investment activity, which increase labor and capital supplies. Mitchell refers to the second hypothesis as a development theory, because it is based on a dynamic model that allows changes in factor supplies, in contrast to the static approach of the trade hypothesis. Development promotes rising wages if growth in the capital stock, due to investment, raises the capital-labor ratio and thereby raises the marginal productivity of labor.

To test the two hypotheses, Mitchell measures the association between growth in the ratio of wages in the nine countries relative to U.S. wages and two variables, the ratio of depreciation per employee relative to the same variable in the United States, and total bilateral trade with the United States (exports plus imports) relative to the foreign country's gross domestic product. Depreciation per worker is a proxy for the capital-labor ratio, to the extent that depreciation is a function of capital stock each period. The results of regressions of relative wages with the depreciation and trade variables in each decade, 1960 to 1980, support the development but not the trade hypothesis. The estimates of the regression coefficients for the depreciation ratio were consistently statistically significant, whereas those of the trade ratio showed no significance.

Although Mitchell makes the important point that variable factor supplies should be incorporated in wage models, his results do not damage the validity of the FPE theorem. Among the several problems with his approach, two basic weaknesses stand out. The first is that Mitchell tests the impact of trade on wage convergence between two countries by measuring the extent of bilateral trade between them. FPE does not depend on a certain threshold level of bilateral trade, however. Wage equalization occurs because product prices have equalized between countries, and that depends on competitive product-markets, not on the volume of trade. Of course, the composition of goods traded and produced by each country also matters, since complete specialization will violate one of the conditions for FPE. Concerning Mitchell's test of the development hypothesis, depreciation is a poor proxy for capital in each country. Direct measurement of capital stock would be a preferred method of estimating the capital-labor ratio, since the relationship between depreciation and the capital stock may not be stable. Capital stock could change through net investment, independent of depreciation expense, for example. Mithell's research is nevertheless an interesting investigation of worldwide wage convergence.

CONTEMPORARY U.S. INTERREGIONAL
WAGE CONVERGENCE

The persistence of regional wage differentials in the United States has attracted a great deal of current research by economists. In particular, southern wages remain lower than the national average and lower than wages in the North. This result is especially surprising in light of vast improvements in labor mobility this century that should have allowed workers to move freely to high-wage regions from low-wage regions, thus tending to equalize regional wages. As in the special case of textile wage differentials discussed earlier, economists have offered several explanations for contemporary regional wage differences, including differences in industry mix, industry wages, cost of living, labor force characteristics, and amenities between regions. U.S. regional wage differentials appear to be narrowing, however, which is an interesting continuation of the wage convergence that took place between the South and the Northeast more than fifty years ago.

Economists have found that part of the observed differences in regional earnings can be attributed to differences in the mix of industries between regions and to interregional differences in wages within the same industry. Lynn E. Browne (1984) investigated the extent to which differences in state average manufacturing wages in 1982 reflected these two sources of wage variation. The lowest average hourly manufacturing earnings that year were found in the South, particularly in Georgia, Mississippi, and the Carolinas. Earnings in the South fell below the national average throughout the period 1973 to 1982. Moreover, the southern states were found to have a higher proportion of low-wage industries in their industrial mix, as well as below-average wages within most industries, compared with the rest of the nation. Thus, below-average wages in the South can be explained by both the types of industries attracted to the region and low wages paid in a single industry (Browne 1984, 45).

Wage differentials that are measured by average hourly or annual earnings of manufacturing workers in nominal (money) terms are subject to adjustment by regional cost-of-living esti- mates. At the extreme, some economists have argued that wage differentials between the North and the South are completely accounted for by a higher cost of living in the North, after con- trolling for the mix of industry within each region. Using three alternative cost-of-living indices published by the Department of Labor, Philip R. P. Coelho and Moheb A. Ghali find that there were no significant differences in real wages between the North and the South in 1967 based on the "intermediate bud- get" cost-of-living index (1973, 762). Although the wage differ- ential persists if either a low- or high-budget cost-of-living in- dex is used to deflate regional wages, they argue that the intermediate index is most appropriate for industrial workers' likely spending patterns (1973, 759). This point remains contro- versial, however; others argue that the cost-of-living adjust- ment only partly explains the nominal wage gap between the North and the South (Ladenson 1973, 754).

Variations in the average wage between regions might also reflect quality differences in the labor force of each region. Rec- ognizing the heterogeneity of labor, the labor force within a region can be described by various characteristics that affect wages, including age, race, and years of formal education. Bel- lante (1979) investigated the mix of labor characteristics in the North and the South based on 1970 census reports of 1969 re- gional earnings of males classified by four age groups, eight educational groups, and two racial groups. In addition, re- gional wages were adjusted by a cost-of-living index that was constructed from city cost-of-living indices formulated by the Bureau of Labor Statistics for intermediate-level budgets in 1969. Bellante concludes that the North-South wage differential in 1969 can be entirely explained by differences in the regional cost of living and mix of labor force characteristics. Specifically, he finds that over 62 percent of the regional earnings gap is due to the higher cost of living in the North and that the remaining 38 percent can be attributed to differences in the age, schooling, and racial mix of labor in each region (1979, 173).

Since some economists continue to find wage differentials even after accounting for industry-mix, cost-of-living, and labor-mix differences between regions, recent research has investigated the role of local amenities in explaining the remaining differentials. Researchers have compared regional wages of comparable workers, after adjusting for local cost of living to derive real wages. Comparable workers are identified on the basis of gender, years of schooling, years of work experience, race, occupation, and industry, to control for many of the factors that are likely to explain the potential wage differential between any two individuals. The remaining differences in wages will then be due to locational factors.

Gerald A. Carlino (1986) reviews several recent studies that led to the hypothesis concerning locational amenities in explaining regional wage differentials. This research uncovered persistent wage differences between comparable workers in various regions of the United States, even after accounting for cost-of-living differences. Surprisingly, this group of researchers reports that real wages in the South are higher than in other regions, including the North, when wages for individual categories of workers are compared. These economists suggest that the unexplained portion of the wage differentials may be explained by differences in amenities available in different areas. Workers might be willing to accept relatively lower wages in a high-amenity area compared with areas where labor must be compensated to live because the amenities are relatively poor.

Amenities can fall into three main categories: environmental characteristics, local public goods and services, and consumer agglomeration economies (Carlino 1986, 22). Features such as weather and air quality are examples of environmental amenities that vary across locations. Public services include police protection, public parks, and schools, which add to the attractiveness of an area the higher the services relative to the local tax bill. Agglomeration economies refer to the increase in the variety of local goods and services that are offered, the higher the population density of an area.

A number of studies support the view that amenities are reflected in real wages in an inverse relationship. The value of local amenities is difficult to quantify, but statistics such as city size, the crime rate, unemployment rate, and weather data can capture some of the amenities offered within a region. Research suggests that real wages tend to be lower in areas with superior amenities, based on the finding that real wage differentials are essentially eliminated after controlling for these various characteristics of a region (1986, 24). Carlino concludes that while nominal wages differ across regions, and real wages of comparable workers also differ across regions, "when amenities are taken into account . . . real wages do not vary significantly" (1986, 25).

In addition to research explaining the persistence of regional wage differentials, economists have investigated the apparent narrowing of those differentials over time. For example, Browne (1984) notes that although wages in the South remained lowest among the U.S. regions in 1982, "Wages have increased more rapidly in the Carolinas, Virginia and most of the East and West South Central states than in the rest of the country" (1984, 41). Robert Newman (1980) focuses on the convergence in average manufacturing wages between the South and the rest of the nation between 1959 and 1969, based on data from the 1960 and 1970 census reports on earnings for males in manufacturing industries.

Borrowing from the methodology used by Bellante (1979), Newman decomposes the changes in the ratio of wages between the South and the non-South into two categories. Wages may have risen in the South faster than in the rest of the nation because of changes in the composition of the southern labor force relative to the non-South, or because higher wages were paid for the same type of labor attribute. To detect changes in labor characteristics, Newman uses census data on age, race, and years of schooling for the labor force in each region. He then decomposes changes in relative wages into composition effects, which are due to changes in labor attributes, as opposed to wage effects, which are found by controlling for labor characteristics. Newman concludes that southern wages improved relative to the non-South primarily because of higher wages for a given category of labor, rather than because of relative changes in the composition in the regional labor forces. He notes that the question why wages rose in the South remains unanswered by his research, however. Higher wages might reflect improvements in the quality of labor for given categories of workers, or growth in the demand for labor in the

South relative to the non-South could have raised wages regardless of changes in labor quality or composition. To the extent that the quality of southern labor improved, higher wages can be expected to be permanent in the South and the convergence of regional wages should persist. If demand pushed wages up in the South, however, higher wages and interregional wage convergence may be temporary, and may last only as long as industry expansion and labor-demand growth is sustained. Only continued monitoring will reveal whether the recent convergence of regional wages is permanent.

NOTES

1. Differentials were widest for unskilled categories of textile labor (Rook 1979, 4).

2. Southern textile wages rose during the period of the National Industrial Recovery Act (1933–1934), when minimum wages were set in the textile industry, and the North-South differential decreased accordingly (Mansfield 1955, 78).

3. More precisely, real wages would equalize in the absence of migration costs. Both the psychological and monetary costs of relocation would place a wedge between regional wages, thus preventing full equalization.

4. A given proportionate increase in all inputs produces an equal proportionate increase in output; also known as constant returns to scale.

5. Capital costs are equal to the value of capital multiplied by the sum of the depreciation rate plus the interest rate.

6. A number of different techniques can be chosen from a given pool of technological knowledge. For the distinction between technology and technique, and between technological change and technical change, see Feller (1972).

9

The Modern Textile Industry

CURRENT U.S. TEXTILE INDUSTRY

The troubled U.S. textile industry, America's oldest manufacturing activity, is struggling in this decade to survive amid sluggish growth in the demand for textile products and expanded foreign competition. U.S. demand for all textile products has been growing at less than 1 percent annually since the 1970s. Moreover, shipments from cotton weaving mills, one segment of the textile industry, began to decline in the mid-1980s (see Table 9.1). Depressed conditions in the apparel industry have contributed to the textile industry's slowdown.

Textile mills are adjusting to stagnation in the domestic industry by reducing obsolete production capacity and investing in automated machinery to increase labor productivity. Increased merger activity also has promoted further consolidation within the industry. As a result, total industry capacity has expanded little, but capacity utilization has risen substantially.

Domestic production of cotton fabrics consists largely of standardized fabrics that can be produced on a large scale. Over 40 percent of cotton fabrics are print cloth, followed by denims, sheeting, and toweling. Fine fabrics form a very small share of cotton output (see Table 9.2). American manufacturers are now putting a greater emphasis on specialty products, however, because of increased competition from imports in the traditional

Table 9.1
Industry Data: Cotton Weaving Mills

	1982	1983	1984	1985
Value of Shipments (billion $)	$4.0	$4.4	$4.3	$4.2
Employment (000)	76.9	71.6	69.2	65.7
Avg. hourly earnings ($)	$6.44	$6.87	$7.24	$7.41

Source: Department of Commerce."Textiles." 1986 U.S. Industrial Outlook (January 1986): sec. 42, 5.

categories of cotton fabrics. Some firms are turning to automotive fabrics and upholstery products, which are less import-sensitive.

The highest concentration of textile mills remains in the Carolinas and Georgia. North and South Carolina together account for about half of the country's textile employment. Six of the top ten textile-producing states are located in the South. Mills located in Massachusetts now represent just 3 percent of total industry employment.

Table 9.2
Cotton Fabrics Production, 1985

Major Types of Goods	Millions of Square Yards	Share of Total
Print cloth	1,640.5	43%
Denims	688.0	18
Sheeting	485.9	13
Toweling	368.1	10
Fine	192.5	5
Corduroy	172.6	4
Blanketing	109.1	3
Duck	97.7	3
Other	74.9	2
Total	3,849.5	100%

Source: "Textiles, Apparel & Home Furnishings." S&P's Industry Surveys (May 15, 1986): sec. T, 79.

TEXTILE IMPORTS

The trade deficit in textile goods has widened dramatically in recent years. Net imports, found by subtracting textile exports from total imports, jumped to almost $1 billion in 1983 and climbed steadily to over $2.5 billion in 1986 (see Table 9.3). The growth in net imports has been the result of both a steady drop in U.S. textile exports since 1980 and the rapid rise in imports since 1982.

The penetration of foreign-produced textiles is of special concern to the domestic industry. Imports captured 7.2 percent of total textile sales in the United States in 1986, up from 6.5 percent the previous year and 3.7 percent in 1976. Although the import share remains small compared with other industries, such as automobiles or steel, the rapid growth in the share of textiles

Table 9.3
Trade Data: Textile Mill Products (SIC 22)
(in Millions of Dollars)

Year	Value of Imports	Value of Exports	Net Imports
1972	$1,345	$ 603	$ 742
1973	1,423	926	497
1974	1,407	1,284	123
1975	1,107	1,157	-50
1976	1,392	1,399	-7
1977	1,489	1,345	144
1978	1,855	1,466	389
1979	1,834	2,130	-296
1980	2,034	2,488	-454
1981	2,482	2,326	156
1982	2,225	1,766	459
1983	2,557	1,560	997
1984	3,539	1,541	1,998
1985	3,697	1,462	2,235
1986	4,322	1,751	2,571

Source: Department of Commerce. "Textiles." 1987 U.S. Industrial Outlook (January 1987): sec. 42, 1-2.
Note: SIC 22 includes broadwoven and knit fabrics, spun yarns, and carpets and rugs.

from abroad signals increased competition from foreign producers.

The strength of the U.S. dollar in the early–1980s had a negative impact on U.S. textile exports in that period, but subsequent depreciation of the dollar has boosted exports since early 1985. Textile imports have not been dampened by fluctuations in the dollar, however, because most imports come from Asian countries that peg their currency to the dollar. Part of the growth in textile imports may also be due to barriers against textile trade in the European Common Market and Japan, which redirect the products of the developing countries to the relatively freer U.S. market. In addition, domestic producers contend that high domestic cotton prices that are supported by federal farm programs have reduced the international competitiveness of the textile industry, since raw cotton constitutes a large share of production costs.[1]

Japan accounts for 17 percent of U.S. textile imports, followed by Italy, South Korea, China, and Taiwan. As a group, Asian producers now supply about 75 percent of U.S. cotton textile imports, up from 65 percent in 1975 (see Table 9.4).

The U.S. textile industry has been protected from foreign competition to some extent for a number of years. The United States has participated in Multi-Fiber Arrangements (MFA) since 1973, which are designed to shelter the textile industries in industrialized countries from the lower-priced textile exports of developing nations. The MFA establishes a framework for setting textile import controls for the fifty-one countries that belong to the General Agreement on Tariffs and Trade (GATT). The textile and apparel industries are the only ones that are formally exempted from the world trading rules established by GATT. In 1986 the MFA was renewed a fourth time for another five years. In that round of negotiations the scope of the agreement was widened to include new products, such as ramie and silk blends, in addition to cotton, wool, and man-made fibers. The new accord also allows the importing country to impose two-year import restraints, rather than the previous one-year limit.

The MFA provides for the negotiation of bilateral trade agreements between importing and exporting nations to set

Table 9.4

**Sources of U.S. Cotton Textile Imports,* 1975 and 1985
(in Millions of Dollars)**

Country	1975	Share	1985	Share
Canada	$ 3.3	1.4%	$ 10.4	1.2%
Latin America	36.6	15.7	73.3	8.2
Other Western Hemisphere	--	--	0.1	--
Europe	40.1	17.2	128.0	14.3
Japan	19.8	8.5	152.0	17.0
Near East	1.0	0.4	0.6	0.1
South Asia	23.8	10.2	77.3	8.7
Other Asia	107.7	46.2	441.2	49.5
Australia & Oceania	--	--	0.2	--
Africa	0.8	0.3	8.8	1.0
Total	$233.3	100.0%	$892.0	100.0%

Source: U.S. Department of Commerce. "Highlights of U.S. Export and Import Trade (FT990)."
* Woven cotton fabrics, excluding narrow or special fabrics, C.I.F. basis (including cost, insurance, freight).

levels of allowable textile imports, or trade quotas. The United States currently maintains about forty bilateral agreements with textile-producing countries under the MFA. In 1986 U.S. officials reached separate agreements with Japan, Taiwan, Hong Kong, and South Korea to limit the growth of textile and apparel imports from these nations. These four countries account for almost one-half of total U.S. textile and apparel imports. The agreements with Japan and South Korea limit the growth of textile and apparel exports to U.S. markets to less than one percent a year through 1989. The growth of Taiwan's textile imports will be limited to .5 percent annually through 1988. Hong Kong negotiated slightly higher growth rates but agreed to curb exports to the United States through 1991.[2]

The accord with Japan also attempts to curtail evasion of MFA quotas by shipping goods through third countries. The Japanese government will verify the country of origin before releasing textile exports from their ports. The United States hopes to expand such measures with other trading partners to strengthen the MFA framework. In 1985 the U.S. Customs Service introduced new rules directed at the problem of transshipping to avoid textile quotas. Inspectors now must identify the country of origin for textile products entering the United States, rather than identify goods on the basis of where they were processed or completed.

Domestic producers have also benefited from a 1985 law that requires manufacturers to label the country of origin on textile and apparel products that are sold in the United States. That law was a byproduct of the industry's "Crafted with Pride in the U.S.A." campaign to promote a buy-American attitude among U.S. consumers. With U.S.-made garments and fabric more easily identified under the new law, the industry hopes that domestic sales will be boosted by appealing to American patriotism.

With the mounting pressure from imports, domestic mills have been fighting for enhanced legislation to restrict imports of textiles and apparel. Industry leaders argue that the MFA and bilateral agreements have not effectively controlled imports, as evidenced by the doubling in textile imports since the first MFA was negotiated. The industry complains that the agreements are easily evaded and that enforcement is lax. In response to the industry's push for tougher restrictions, textile-state legislators drafted the Textile & Apparel Trade Enforcement Act of 1985, but the Act was vetoed by President Reagan in December 1985, and Congress failed to override the veto in the following summer. The industry continues to campaign for stiffer protectionist measures.

The industry blames imports for the significant loss of jobs in the textile sector. Textile employment has dropped from one million in the early–1970s to about 700,000 in 1985. In the domestic cotton weaving mills, employment has been cut 15 percent since 1982, to 66,000 in 1985. Proponents of textile restrictions equate the growth in imports with plant closings and lost jobs.

Recent research has challenged the case for restricting textile imports, however. Richard B. McKenzie (1986) studied the impact of import growth on both the textile and the apparel industries. While apparel imports had a negative impact on employment in that sector, textile imports have not been a statistically significant factor in textile job losses between 1960 and 1985. McKenzie argues that textile employment losses can be attributed to productivity improvements, rather than import competition.

First, McKenzie shows that even if past textile imports had been replaced with domestic products, textile employment would have declined by about the same amount between 1973 and 1984. Although textile employment would have risen each year to produce the equivalent amount of textile products at home, changes in total employment would not have been affected much. He found that employment would have risen by about 50,000 in both 1973 and 1984 had imports been supplied domestically, but that employment still would have declined by the same as the actual figure, nearly 300,000. The hypothetical decline would have been almost as great as the actual in the period between 1980 and 1984 as well. In other words, replacing imports with domestic production would have raised the level of employment but would not have altered the pattern of changes in the employment figures in this period.

McKenzie next developed a regression model to analyze the impact of productivity change, real textile and apparel imports, and real disposable personal income on domestic textile employment. The model is estimated over the period 1960 to 1984, using annual data. The results suggest that domestic productivity improvements in the textile industry have had a statistically significant negative influence on employment. McKenzie estimates that a 1 percent increase in textile productivity can be expected to lead to a .46 percent reduction in textile employment. He finds that in the 1980 to 1984 period, the 21 percent increase in worker productivity in the textile industry during the period led to 80 percent of the actual employment loss. Between 1973 and 1984 labor productivity increased 49 percent, accounting for 85 percent of the loss of 264,000 textile jobs in that period.

The regression estimates of the coefficients for the import variables were also significant. Textile imports were associated with gains in textile employment, which suggests that lower-priced imports may have benefited domestic producer to the extent that foreign goods were inputs in a domestic production process. Apparel imports had a negative correlation with textile employment, which is consistent with the expected substitution effect that foreign apparel products would have on both domestic apparel and textile goods. For equal dollar imports of textile and apparel products, however, the gains from the textile imports would more than offset the losses from the apparel imports.

Real disposable personal income was positively associated with employment gains in this period, and the regression estimates were statistically significant. This result was anticipated, since a higher income would stimulate the demand for textile products and, in turn, textile employment.

In summary, McKenzie's results point to two interesting conclusions. No support was found for the claim that textile imports are associated with employment declines in the textile industry. Moreover, two potential sources for the recent job losses in the textile industry appear to be productivity increases and apparel imports. The impact of apparel imports would be offset by the positive impact of textile imports, however. Since apparel restrictions are usually formulated in tandem with restrictions on textile imports, these results support the greater liberalization of apparel and textile imports to the United States. Although productivity increases have contributed to employment losses in the industry, on balance the industry has gained from increased profitability that can probably be traced to those productivity gains.

AUTOMATION

The domestic mills have responded to intensified foreign competition by installing labor-saving equipment to increase productivity and thereby cut production costs. The domestic mills have steadily increased capital expenditures since the late–1970s to modernize and automate textile production processes. In recent years over 80 percent of the industry's retained earnings have been directed to capital spending. Spending on new machinery averaged $1.5 billion in the past ten years. Capital spending hit a record $2 billion in the industry in 1984, although it eased somewhat in the following two years.

Improvements in textile machinery have continued to advance since the days of the revolutionary ring spindle and automatic loom. Spinning is now done in a one-step process called open-end spinning, which integrates the spinning and winding of yarn into one operation. Open-end spinning produces five times the output of ring spinning, makes a better quality yarn, and requires fewer operators per machine. Air-jet spinning and friction spinning are currently under development and promise to allow further improvements in speed and quality in the spinning process.

The shuttleless loom is gradually replacing the traditional shuttle loom. The new looms use jets of water or air, rather than shuttles, to weave cloth. The shuttleless loom operates at three times the speed of the traditional models. According to the American Textile Manufacturers Institute, about 40 percent of domestic looms now in use are shuttleless. The state-of-the-art looms are now all foreign-made, so domestic mills are completely dependent on looms made in Japan and Europe.

At other stages of textile production, the advances in machinery have been just as rapid as in spinning and weaving. Robots are now used to unload raw cotton and transfer cotton and yarn to different areas of the plant, guided by computer. Driverless carts deliver materials inside the plant. Bale-O-Matics pick fixed amounts of cotton from the bales to feed into the cleaning machines. The most modern plants are computer-integrated, so that the entire plant is monitored by a system that controls the flow of production from the unloading of raw cotton to the finishing of woven fabrics. Computers also constantly monitor the efficiency of the spinning and weaving machines and can dispatch a cart when the yarn supply is low.

The advances in textile machinery have been accompanied by substantial improvements in mill productivity. Martin Neil Bailey and Alok K. Chakrabarti (1985) point to the textile industry as an example of a sector where innovations were a source of productivity growth in the 1970s. They cite the evidence that as the number of textile equipment innovations per year rose from 135 in the period 1967 to 1973 to 141 in the period 1974 to

1979, productivity growth in the industry rose from 2.73 percent per year in the first period to 3.56 percent per year in the second period.

More recent figures indicate that the growth in textile productivity has been relatively high among domestic industries. Output per worker increased 5 percent annually in the past ten years, compared with only 2.1 percent annually on average for all manufacturing industries. In addition to generating more output per worker, the new technology has reduced manufacturing costs by reducing the labor content in production. In a fully automated plant, labor's share of manufacturing costs drops to only 10 percent, compared with 50 percent in a traditional plant.

The introduction of high technology to American mills has also improved product quality. In 1980 the textile industry produced fabric with an average twenty-five flaws in every 100 linear yards, whereas in 1985 imperfections were reduced to fewer than eight per 100 yards of cloth.

OUTLOOK FOR U.S. TEXTILE INDUSTRY

The domestic textile industry will benefit in the near term from efforts to cut manufacturing costs by automating textile production, and further improvements in textile machinery that will increase mill efficiency are on the horizon. The trend toward consolidation of production capacity is also helping to increase productivity by eliminating less-efficient operations. Moreover, the industry is becoming more cost-competitive on the world market because of the steady depreciation of the dollar against major currencies since early 1985, which will aid the export of U.S. textile products.

Sales of domestic cotton textile products may receive a boost from the growing popularity of natural cotton fabrics, now that consumer tastes appear to be swinging back to cotton from man-made fibers for the first time in two decades. Per-capita consumption of cotton peaked in the early–1960s and then began to decline as preferences shifted to polyester and other man-made fabrics. In addition to regained popularity, advertising and promotion by the cotton industry and lower cotton prices are likely to raise domestic consumption of cotton. New weaving techniques that have improved cotton's wearability, and the development of techniques for blending cotton and polyester fibers have also raised the cotton content in many fabrics.

Further declines in textile employment are likely, as mills make greater use of labor-saving equipment, such as the shuttleless loom and robots. Analysts expect industry employment to decline 3 percent annually, on average, in coming years. The decline in the textile labor force will be accompanied by higher mill profitability, however, since the layoffs will stem primarily from automation, rather than from the expected growth in imports. Imports are not likely to be contained by the new global textile agreement, in light of the many loopholes, and the industry's push for tougher protectionist legislation is likely to continue to be blocked by the Reagan administration. The next administration may be more receptive to textile import restraints, however.

In the longer term, today's domestic textile industry will probably be displaced by production in the developing economies. U.S. competitiveness in the world markets is likely to be further eroded, as low-wage Asian and Latin American countries gain the technology and experience to match the U.S. level of productivity in textile production. The domestic industry, much like the pre-1930 northern U.S. mills, has been slow to modernize relative to other countries. Traditional models still make up the majority of U.S. textile equipment in use today. Domestic mills are replacing the older models, but remain at a disadvantage compared with newly established textile industries in developing countries that rely entirely on the newest equipment.

RELOCATION PATTERN

The relocation of textile production has followed a recurrent pattern since the British textile mills lost supremacy in the industry in the nineteenth century. Textile manufacturing has continued to shift from industrialized economies, to emerge in relatively low-wage, newly industrializing regions. The center of textile production has moved from Britain in the eighteenth century, to the northeastern United States in the early nineteenth century, and then to Japan, India, and the southern United States. With the emergence of textile industries in several developing nations, the U.S. textile industry will probably suffer the same fate as the British and northern U.S. textile mills.

The shift of production from industrailzed to developing nations was the focus of a 1965 study that was conducted under the auspices of the GATT (Cotton Textiles Committee 1966). The study surveys the major developments in production and trade in cotton textiles during the first three years of the 1962 "Long-Term Arrangement Regarding International Trade in Cotton Textiles." One of the main objectives of the arrangement was to promote textile exports from less-developed countries. The most important trend identified by the study is that the developing countries figured more prominently in growth of textile activity than the industrialized nations. More specifically, the committee found that a decline in cotton textile production in the industrialized countries between 1953 and 1964 was more than offset by growth in the production of textiles in the developing countries. The decline in production in the industrialized countries was accompanied by an increase in imports. Although the combined production of cotton textiles of the industrialized countries remained greater than in the developing countries, the share of world production represented by the developed countries declined steadily between 1953 and 1964. As the less-developed countries produced an increasing share of the world's cotton yarn and fabrics, their share of world exports of those goods also increased.[3]

The study also noted a number of structural changes in world textile production taking place in the early 1960s. In many countries textile firms were expanding through vertical and horizontal integration, and massive capital investment was directed at modernizing textile production capacity. Adoption of modern technology, including advanced machinery and new techniques, was raising output per machine and per machine-hour. The committee found wide variations in productivity improvements among both industrialized and developing countries, however.

Investment in the industrialized countries in this period was directed at raising production efficiency rather than increasing capacity or the level of production. Obsolete equipment was scrapped and replaced with advanced machinery, which reduced the labor cost per unit of output because of higher labor and machinery productivity but resulted in declines in total production capacity. By contrast, capital investment in the developing nations provided additional equipment that raised total capacity and also increased the demand for labor. Investment focused on purchases of skilled-labor-saving equipment that made use of these countries' abundant supply of unskilled labor.

Total world textile production capacity declined because of the trimming of the industrialized countries' capacity between 1953 and 1964. Along with the decline in the world's stock of cotton textile spindles and looms, the location of that machinery also shifted. The buildup of textile machinery in the developing countries with the contraction in the industrialized countries' machinery stock caused a shift in the concentration of world textile capacity to the less-developed countries.[4]

Of particular interest is the study's observation that the gap in textile wages between developing and industrialized countries had narrowed over the period from 1953 to 1964. Textile wage levels in some of the developing economies grew at a faster rate than in the developed countries, but textile wages remained lower in the developing nations.[5] The committee notes that low wages do not necessarily translate to low wage costs because of possible differences in labor productivity between countries, but precise comparisons of wage costs were not made for various technical reasons.

The study predicted accurately that less-developed countries would continue to expand their presence in the world textile industry. In spite of higher capital requirements in the industry because of technological advances in textile machinery, the industry remains well-suited to production in an unskilled–labor-abundant country. In addition, industrialized countries would increase their specialization in novelty goods and specialties, according to the study. The same trends identified in this GATT study over twenty years ago can be observed in the world textile industry today.

World textile production has tended to shift to newly industrializing countries because textile manufacturing traditionally
has been one of the first industries to be established in a developing economy. Raymond Vernon (1966) attributes this pattern of industrial relocation to the standardization of textile
products, a theory he formalizes in his "product cycle" hypothesis. Product standardization occurs in the final stages of product development, which begins with introduction of the new
product to the marketplace and proceeds along the stages of its
product cycle. Once the market for a good expands such that
production can be conducted on a mass scale, the producer's
focus shifts from concern about product characteristics to that
of production costs. Large-scale production encourages capital
investment in labor-saving equipment, which typically becomes economical at a high volume of production.

Vernon points out that "Standardized textile products are, of
course, the illustration par excellence of the sort of product that
meets the criteria" of goods that are likely to be manufactured
and exported by the less-developed countries. Such standardized goods will require significant inputs of labor, be suited for
production in a remote area, and have a high price elasticity of
demand, so that they sell largely on the basis of price. Other
products that fit this description are steel, simple fertilizers and
newsprint (1966, 204).

Once textile production became automated in the late nineteenth century, it was particularly suited to capital-scarce, labor-abundant regions. The industry is also more easily introduced to developing areas, which are typically skilled-labor
scarce, because modern textile machinery requires a shorter
training period than other mechanized production. Textile
manufacturing capability is considered so important to development that the United Nations made recommendations in the
1960s to work with other agencies to promote textile production in developing countries and to assist in plant establishment, training, and modernization of existing plants (UNIDO
1969).

Industry relocation is usually a prolonged process, however,
in spite of the evident low-wage advantage in the developing
region or country. Based on the history of the early–twentieth-

century U.S. industry, the older textile center adapts to the new competitors by seeking market niches and continuing to update equipment. The most efficient established mills remain competitive, despite higher wages, during the intermediate period of growth in textile production in the newer region. The current U.S. textile industry may continue to prosper during this period of transition in world textile production. Eventually, however, only a few specialty mills are likely to survive competition from foreign textile producers.

NOTES

1. Domestic producers will benefit from the gradual dismantling of agricultural price supports provided by the Food Security Act of 1985, however. The 1985 farm bill is designed to increase the competitiveness of the U.S. farm sector by setting certain crop prices at the world price to spur U.S. crop exports. Cotton prices have begun to fall since implementation of the new policy, which will help the domestic textile industry.

2. The United States also reached an agreement with India to limit the growth of textile exports to 6 percent between 1987 and 1990 and is currently negotiating with China to restrict textile exports from that country.

3. The industrialized countries' share of world production of yarn dropped from 47 percent in 1953 to 35 percent in 1964, and that group's share of world fabric production dropped from 47 percent to 36 percent in the same period. The industrialized nations exported 35 percent of total world yarn exports in 1964, down from 66 percent in 1953, and their share of fabric exports dropped to 32 percent in 1964 from 55 percent in 1953 (Cotton Textiles Committee 1966, 15).

4. In 1939, 66 percent of the world's spindles and 59 percent of looms were located in the industrialized countries. By 1964 those shares dropped to 40 percent and 38 percent, respectively (Cotton Textiles Committee 1966, 43).

5. This pattern of wage convergence in the world textile industry is consistent with the worldwide manufacturing wage convergence that was noted in Chapter 8.

Conclusion

10

This study presents a new approach for investigating the process of the American textile relocation and subsequent equalization of regional textile wages. To gain an understanding of the southern textile expansion and the northern decline between 1880 and 1930, this research focuses on changes in individual mills. Textile directories contain a wealth of information that census data obscure by reporting statistics at an aggregated level. Although previous studies utilized textile directories to some extent, the present work makes greater use of the data available in those records. The primary contribution of this research is the study of mill survival in the industry, which the directory listings make possible by providing a record of each mill's years of operation during this period.

This source is especially informative for the study of the southern textile industry, since so little is known about the details of southern textile production. Southern mill records are rare, and it is difficult to generalize about the entire region based on the few comprehensive mill records that are available. Even in the case of the northern mills, which have far better historical records, the mill directories provide detailed information about a far greater number of mills than in other studies.

The mill directories provide evidence about the pace of the relocation, the strategies followed by the surviving mills in each region, and the role of textile machinery innovations in the development of the industry. In the regional comparison of the U.S. textile industry, both census data and individual mill data reveal that the relocation was not immediate. The industry continued to grow in both regions for over forty years after its introduction in the South, although at a much faster rate in the South. The northern industry remained viable during this period of relocation, as evidenced by the growth in new mills and the substantial proportion of surviving northern mills before 1920. The collapse of the northern industry did not become visible until the early 1920s, when the number of mills began to decline sharply.

The regional branches of the industry were quite distinct. Apparently, the strategies for survival varied between the regions. The production technique, indicated by capital intensity and type of machinery used, differed between the two regions, which was consistent with the disparity in regional factor price ratios. The larger mill capital values and higher capital-labor ratios found in the northern mills corresponded to the relatively low interest rates and rental rates in the North, and to the higher wage-rental rate ratio compared with the South.

The surviving and nonsurviving mills were compared both on the basis of descriptive statistics and regression analysis of the factors that may have affected mill performance. The surviving mills in both regions were larger, newer, and adopted new equipment models to a greater extent than the mills that failed. The regression analysis of growth in mill capacity indicated that spindle growth was higher the larger the mill, whether size is measured by capital or total spindles. This suggests that economies of scale or other advantages to larger size aided mill growth in each region.

The regression of the relationship between the probability of mill survival and several mill characteristics suggests that the strategy of the mills in the North was to modernize and shift production to higher grades of output. Northern mills were able to remain competitive with the new southern mills by investing in new technology, as measured by the adoption of the ring spindle in the mills, and by seeking market niches that southern mills had not yet entered.

The directory data provide a basis for studying the role of

textile machinery innovations in the process of the industry re-location. Since the use of the ring and mule spindles is documented for a large proportion of the mills listed in the directories, the adoption of the new ring spindle could be estimated. After 1900 almost every southern mill in the study used only the ring spindle. Surviving southern mills had a slightly higher average ring-spindle ratio than the nonsurviving mills, although both ratios were high. Since the ring was so prevalent in the South, the variable measuring the adoption of the ring spindle could not be estimated in regression analysis.

Among northern mills, however, the use of the ring during the earlier half of the period studied was associated with mill survival to 1930. Surviving northern mills had a higher average ring-spindle ratio compared with mills that failed, and the regression estimate for the ring-share variable had a statistically significant positive association with the probability of mill survival.

The adoption of the ring spindle is explored in greater depth by analyzing the link between spindle choice and various mill features. A link is found between use of the ring and the type of output produced and mill age, based on the directory evidence. The slower adoption of the ring spindle in the North was clearly associated with the production of fine output in that region. Northern mills that produced fine yarn used mule spindles to a greater extent than mills producing lower grades of yarn. In the South, however, ring use was so extensive that grade of output did not appear to influence the choice of spindle.

Mill age appeared to be related to the choice of spindle. When mills were categorized according to age, the oldest and newest mills each year had the highest proportion of ring spindles to total mill spindles in both the North and the South. A new mill probably favored the ring spindle because the total costs of production were lower using a ring than a mule spindle. An older mill was likely to be replacing worn equipment, so its decision was essentially the same as that of the new mill. An intermediate mill likely had mule spindles in place, especially if the mill was equipped pre-1900, before the ring spindle was available. A mill with installed spindles may have found that production costs were lower by postponing a switch to ring spindles, since the large capital expenditure may have offset the labor-saving advantages of the ring spindle.

Regional factor prices probably also played a role in the type of spindle used in each region, since factor prices would have determined the production costs with alternative spindle techniques. Since production costs and input prices were not included in the directories, a model for spindle choice is presented that illustrates the relationship between factor prices and the type of spindle used in production. The model predicts that rising wages and declining interest rates would have favored the use of the ring spindle in textile production, which is consistent with the experience in the American textile industry in the early twentieth century.

The finding that adoption of the ring spindle contributed to mill survival in each region supports the hypothesis that technological changes in textile machinery facilitated the shift of the industry to the South before 1930. This hypothesis holds that skilled-labor-saving technological improvements led to the introduction of the textile industry in the South, and that further refinements in the machinery allowed southern production to shift to a wider range of textile output and dominate the industry. Use of the ring spindle apparently promoted the competitiveness of textile mills, judging by the analysis of mill survival. Therefore, adoption of technological advances played a role in the relocation of the industry. While developments in the capital markets and improvements in labor quality may have been relevant to the relocation process as well, these alternative hypotheses could not be confirmed or denied based on the evidence from the textile directories.

This study is also concerned with the convergence of regional textile wages during the period of industry relocation. Low wages in the South played a major role in motivating the shift of textile production to that region by 1930. Although that wage gap was closed to some extent over time, southern wages remained lower than in the North throughout the period and continue to lag behind wages in the rest of the nation even today.

Historians continue to debate the origins of the interregional wage differentials before 1930. A number of explanations have been offered, including a lower cost of living in the South, lower productivity among southern workers, and various labor-market imperfections that might have prevented interregional wage equality in nominal (money) wages. Productivity differences and structural differences in regional labor markets could result in differences in real wages between the North and the South. The real-wage differences would imply differences in the observed nominal wages. Differences in cost of living between the two regions, however, result in differences in nominal (money) wages even though real wages might be equal.

The study of regional wage differentials in this early period should be approached with caution, however, since historical wage data in this industry are likely to be deficient. Incomplete data as well as measurement errors reduce the reliability of textile wage statistics before 1930. Historical price data used in calculating regional cost of living are also of limited value, because of insufficient records and inconsistencies in the available data. The various explanations for apparent real- and nominal-wage differentials before 1930 remain unsettled because of problems with the historical wage data.

This study borrows from the literature of international trade to offer a fresh approach to the question of historical textile-wage differentials. In particular, the "factor price equalization" (FPE) theorem is relevant to the convergence of northern and southern textile wage between 1880 and 1930. The theorem demonstrates that under certain conditions wages would equalize even though labor was immobile between regions. The fundamental conditions for this theorem to hold include competitive factor and product markets, homogeneous factors between regions, and incomplete specialization in each region.

In the late nineteenth century, however, conditions for FPE were probably violated. In particular, the concentration of southern production in agriculture violated the condition for nonspecialization. Industrial development in the South after 1880 meant that the conditions for wage equalization under this theorem were better satisfied. That textile wages between the North and the South began to equalize by 1930 confirms the FPE theorem. The FPE model predicts the timing and pattern of regional wage equalization that we observe between 1880 and 1930. This result is in sharp contrast to the typical explanations of North-South wage differentials in this period.

This detailed study of the American textile industry relocation provides some insight into the ongoing relocation of world textile production. One is struck by the number of similarities between the current trends in world textile production and the earlier case of U.S. textile relocation. Today's southern domestic mills are now in the position of the early–twentieth-century northern mills, as they struggle to remain viable in the increasingly competitive world textile market.

The U.S. industry is currently pursuing strategies reminiscent of the ill-fated North, including a shift to new product lines and modernization of domestic plants. The introduction of highly automated textile equipment has prolonged the life of the domestic industry by increasing labor productivity and reducing labor costs. The industry has also experienced considerable consolidation through trimmed capacity, mergers, and attrition.

Today's Asian mills have the advantages enjoyed by the early southern mills, including low wages and more modern equipment. As in the case of the American textile industry relocation, technological changes in textile production have facilitated the shift of production to less-developed economies. Mills in the new textile centers can equip the plants with the latest models of automated textile machinery and are ahead of the U.S. mills in the adoption of new textile technology. Older U.S. plants rationally postpone the switch to the expensive high-technology equipment while installed machinery remains operative. As in the North before 1930, U.S. mills are likely to continue to modernize, but will lag behind the rate of innovation in the newer industrial regions.

If a parallel is drawn to the case of the U.S. textile relocation, newly industrializing nations may be expected to emerge as the new centers of world textile production, while textile production in industrialized countries declines. The relocation process can be slow, however. Both the mature and new industries are likely to continue to expand in the intermediate phase of the

relocation. If the earlier U.S. experience in textile industry relocation to the low-wage South can serve as a guide, foreign
producers in these developing nations are likely to become the
dominant force in world textile production.

Appendix A
Data Collection and Special Problems

Data from the Davison's Textile Blue Books, published annually by the Davison Publishing Company, have been recorded for cotton textile mills in Massachusetts and North Carolina. A second directory, the Official American Textile Directory, was used to supplement incomplete listings in the Davison's directory. Directories for 1885, 1895, 1900, 1905, 1910, 1914–1915, 1919, 1925, and 1930–1931 have been recorded. The period covered by a given year begins in July of that year, through July of the next year.

The study excludes mills that were idle and those producing knits, small cotton wares (which include thread, cordage, tapes, webbings, shoelaces, embroideries, braid, twine, and clotheslines), elastic, cotton waste, or mattresses. The total number of mills included over the entire forty-five-year period is 683 in North Carolina and 350 in Massachusetts. Multiple plants of the same company were combined in one listing if they were operating in the same city. A mill was included even if no data were reported that year (in other words, only the mill name and location were listed), since the record of a mill's existence was important in establishing industry survivors and in estimating mill age.

The variables recorded for each mill are the following:

1. Mill code (1 to 716 for North Carolina mills, and 1,001 to 1,361 for Massachusetts mills. This allows region to be determined in the computer program by the mill code. For example, southern mills can be selected on the basis of a mill code of less than 1,000).
2. Capital, current dollar value.
3. Number of employees.
4. Number of spindles, equal to the sum of ring and mule spindles (in cases where the type of spindle was indicated).
5. Number of ring spindles.
6. Number of mule spindles.
7. Number of looms.
8. City population.
9. Source of power, coded by B, W, or E, where B = boiler or steam, W = water wheel, and E = electricity.
10. Year, a three-digit value (885 to 930).
11. Output, coded A to Z:
    For mills producing both yarn and cloth, only the cloth output was recorded. A mill specializing in spinning was identified by the fact that it reported no looms, and mills specializing in weaving reported no spindles and usually noted that yarn was purchased.
    a. Yarn output was coded Y = yarn, followed by C = coarse, for counts between 0 and 19, M = medium, for counts between 20 and 39, or F = fine, for counts 40 and above.
    b. Cloth output was coded with one or more of the following:
        A = sheeting
        B = gingham
        D = denim, duck, or broadcloth
        E = cheviot
        G = chambray, lawn, or organdy
        H = ticking
        I = corduroy
        J = madras
        K = sateen
        L = flannel
        N = towel
        O = upholstery or bedspreads
        P = blankets
        Q = bagging or osnaburg
        R = plaid, checks, or stripes
        S = twill or dobby weaves

T = colored
U = outing
V = damask or linen
W = drill
X = print or calico
Z = domet
F = fine or fancy

Fine output was defined in the study as the codes F (in either yarn or cloth), G, J, or K.

The directory listing included additional facts that were not coded directly for the data set used in the empirical portion of the study, but were recorded in separate notes for each mill. Those data include the mill name, year of establishment, names of the mill management, the selling agent, location of any branches of the same company, and the city and county where the mill was located. This information was useful for clarifying problems of inconsistency in the directory listings.

In the cases where a mill was not listed in the same city in successive directories, one city was determined to be best. A state map was checked to confirm that a mill did not relocate when this inconsistency ocurred. It was usually the case that the mill had substituted the nearest railroad station or post office in place of the actual location when the city listing changed.

Information about a mill's relationship to a parent company or consolidation with other mills helped to clarify incongruities in the reporting of mill capital, which might appear excessive if the mill listed the corporation's total capital stock rather than that mill's share. In those cases the capital value was recorded as a missing value in the data set for each of the mills affiliated with that corporation.

Mill name changes occurred for various reasons. The same mill code was retained if the name was changed from the name of one of the mill officers, which suggested that a family-owned mill had gone public. A new code was used if the mill was taken over by some other company or merged with another mill to create a third mill. The assignment of a new code meant that the original mill would be treated as a nonsurvivor in the study. Cases of acquisitions or mergers created the potential problem of mislabeling a viable mill as one that was not successful prior to 1930. Lacking background information on the circumstances of most of the takeovers and mergers, however, we do not know the financial conditions of the mills involved. (The dates of the takeovers and mergers in the following discussion are approximated, because the directories used in this study were selected at five-year intervals.)

There were few cases of takeovers or mergers in the data, which minimizes the problem of misclassifying nonsurviving mills whose names changed following the mergers. In Massachusetts there were six reported takeovers by a new entrant to the industry, one each in 1910 and 1915, and two each in 1925 and 1930. New mills were created in each instance, which meant that the six mills acquired were treated as nonsurvivors in the study. Half of these takeovers involved changes in the former mill, in size or type of output, so it is safe to assume that the mills that were taken over did go out of business. All mills but one were much smaller than the average northern mill that year, which supports the suspicion that the mills did fail. Of the takeovers occurring before 1930, only one survived to 1930, so most of the mills involved in takeovers would not have qualified as survivors in any case. The estimated length of operation and mill age in the study would have been longer, however.

There were seven cases of mergers in Massachusetts, which occurred when two former mills combined to create a new mill or when one mill merged with another existing mill. Two of the mergers took place in 1919 (neither survived to 1930) and the rest in 1930. Of these seven mergers, one involved a merger with an existing mill, four were cases where the mills formed an association (Berkshire Fine Spinning Association), and the other two joined the large firm, B. B. Knight (which was acquired by the Consolidated Textile Corporation of New York City in 1920). In each case the mills appeared to operate unchanged (in all but their name). It could be argued that these seven mills ought to be classified as survivors (although the merger probably introduced new management to the mill), but the numbers involved are so few that it is unlikely to have biased the results of the study in any case. At least some of the mergers were known to have rescued failing mills, however. For example, the Berkshire Fine Spinning Associates merger absorbed two fine-goods mills that were going to liquidate (Kennedy 1936, 66–67).

There were more cases of takeovers and mergers in North Carolina, but a smaller share of total mills was involved compared with Massachusetts. In North Carolina thirteen cases of takeovers were reported, three in 1910, two in 1919, two in 1925, and six in 1930. New firms were introduced in each case. Four of the takeovers occurring before 1930 survived to 1930, while three did not. Out of all thirteen takeovers, seven kept the same mill size following the change in ownership (and of these, three kept the same type of output). The remaining six increased spindle capacity, doubling the mill's total spindle stock in most cases. Most of these mills were smaller than the average southern mill, as in the northern takeovers, so it is likely that the mills were failing and that the change in ownership is appropriately treated as the creation of a new mill.

Most of the eighteen mergers in North Carolina occurred in the 1920s. There were two mergers in 1910, seven in 1925, and nine in 1930. One involved a merger with an existing parent mill. Four mills became part of the northern Consolidated Textile Corporation, which was formed in 1919, and the remaining thirteen cases created new mills following the merger. Of the nine mergers before 1930, eight survived to 1930 (the one failure was a 1925 merger). The mills that merged were all smaller than the average southern mill, and half of these remained the same size following the merger. As noted earlier, treating these mills as nonsurvivors even though there was no apparent physical change in the plant may be improper, but the potential bias is small. In the remaining eleven cases the merger created mills larger than the participating mills prior to the merger, and in three of these cases, the new mills were among the largest in the South with a spindle capacity of over 100,000 spindles.

Since location of any existing branches is indicated in the mill directory listing, sets of mills that represent branches of a common parent company could be identified. The cases of interregional branching from the North to the South are especially interesting as evidence of direct investment from the capital-abundant North. Direct investment accomplished the transfer of capital between regions at a time when the regional capital markets were underdeveloped and has been viewed as a means of circumventing the barriers to capital mobility that existed in the financial capital markets of the period (Davis 1965).

Nine Massachusetts mills established branches in the South before 1930. These nine northern mills did not conform to a specific pattern, however. Five were larger than the average Massachusetts mill and four were smaller. Four had mule spindles, which all four removed after 1919, and five had none. Three of the mills produced fine output, and only two mills produced more than one type of output. The majority of northern mills that expanded to the South concentrated their northern production in coarse and medium grades of textiles, which were better suited to southern production than fine output (especially earlier in the period).

The size of the northern mill appears to have been related to the timing of its expansion to the South. The mills with larger than average capital had southern branches prior to 1920, whereas those with smaller than average capital did not establish a southern branch until the 1920s. Perhaps a large mill could take on the risk involved in entering the South before the southern mills had proven that the textile industry was viable in that region. After all, the southern takeover of the industry was not apparent until after 1920, when the first signs of collapse of the northern industry emerged. The average capital stock of the mills branching to the South was $3.6 million, and the average number of spindles was 106,000, which were both greater than in the average Massachusetts mill. The survival rate of these mills was similar to that of the other Massachusetts mills—five out of the nine mills survived to 1930, which was a survival rate of 56 percent.

Only two of those branches were in North Carolina, which limits information about the southern branches of these northern mills. Judging by the branches in North Carolina, the northern parent mill did not set up mills in the South that replicated production in the North. The North Carolina branches produced only yarn and were similar in size to the typical southern mill.

Seventeen mills in the North Carolina sample were branches of northern companies that were located elsewhere than in Massachusetts. The survival rate for these mills was quite high—twelve of the branches were operating in 1930 (two were new that year). The survival rate, not including the new mills, was 67 percent, higher than the average southern mill. As a group these mills were larger than the average southern mill, judging by average spindles. Eight had smaller spindle stocks than the average southern mill, while seven had larger, but the total spindles in one mill was about ten times the size of the average southern mill. Of the five nonsurviving mills, all but one were quite small relative to the average southern mill. For all but one of these branches, the mills were typical of southern mills and small relative to their northern parent mills. This is further evidence that the northern mills adapted the production parameters of their southern branches to those typical of southern, not northern, operations. A number of factors might have constrained the size of these branches, including regional factor prices, a higher risk of operating in the South, and limited working capital of the northern parent mill.

A number of southern and northern mills in the sample were branches of parent companies that were located in the same region. About 10 percent of mills in each region were intraregional branches—33 of the 350 Massachusetts mills and 61 of the 683 North Carolina mills. The southern mills that were branches were on average 50 percent larger than the average southern mill, based on spindle capacity. Twelve of these mills, or 20 percent, were new in 1930, which is 5 percentage points more than the share of new mills in 1930 for all southern mills. Excluding the new mills, the survival rate of the southern branches was 71 percent, approximately the same as for all southern mills. It may be that mills belonging to a common parent company had an advantage in greater access to capital or a larger management staff, which is consistent with the larger size of the average branch. But the normal survival rate for the branches suggests that the branches ultimately fared no better than the independent mills in the South.

The evidence of the northern mills that were related to another northern company shows that they were on average smaller and had a lower survival rate by 10 percentage points than other northern mills. The branches had about 5,000 fewer spindles than the average northern mill. Four of the branches, or 12 percent, were new in 1930, about the same share of all northern mills that were new that year. Excluding the new mills, the branches had a 45 percent survival rate, compared to 52 percent for all northern mills in 1919 and 58 percent in 1925. The branching phenomenon in the North appears to have been a poor choice for a mill, judging by the lower survival rate, but there is not enough information in the directory data to indicate why.

Appendix B
Overview of Textile Production since 1800

This appendix describes the major developments in the manufacture of cotton textile products following the eighteenth-century Industrial Revolution, when the industry was first organized under a factory system. Although there were earlier cases of textile operations collected under one roof, the Industrial Revolution marks the beginning of the mill system. Before that time, the textile industry had evolved to a sophisticated craft but remained a cottage industry. The earliest evidence of textile work dates from Neolithic cultures of about 5,000 B.C., and use of cotton fibers in textile production was popular in ancient Egypt and in India by 3,000 B.C.

The technological developments in textile production that were made in the eighteenth century were based on the application of engineering and physical principles. Mechanical improvements in this period increased the speed of textile production and vastly raised the productivity of each textile worker. Beginning in the late nineteenth century, the growth of scientific knowledge about textile fibers led to the application of chemical properties to textile processing. A greater understanding about the structure and properties of fibers allowed textile manufacturers to improve the quality of their products and expand the varieties of fabrics they could produce. The discovery of man-made fibers opened new markets for the industry and led to the application of new processes to traditional fibers as well.

The development of electronics and computers in the twentieth century produced further leaps in the speed and precision of textile machinery. The discovery of new engineering, physical, chemical, and electronic principles has enhanced the research and development efforts of the modern textile industry. As a result, the industry continues to make rapid advances in the development of new fibers, processes to improve textile characteristics, and testing methods that allow greater quality control.

Textile production occurs in five major steps: preparatory processes, spinning, spooling, weaving, and finishing. The first step in preparing the raw cotton begins by opening the bales of cotton. Cotton from a number of bales is mixed and loosened up in the bale breaker, a machine that replaced hand labor in the late nineteenth century. Blowers force the cotton through a large pipe to the opener, or automatic feeder. There it is further blended with cotton from different lots to obtain a uniform length, diameter, density, and moisture content in the yarn that will later be produced. In some mills a picking machine separates and shakes the cotton fibers, to remove twigs and dirt which are commonly found in natural fibers. Opening and picking may be combined in the same machine.

The next step in the preparatory process is carding, a process of separating and straightening the individual fibers; remaining impurities are also removed. The carding machine produces a thick, untwisted rope called "sliver." The most significant advancement in carding was the invention of the revolving flat card by the British in the nineteenth century. The important features of the new card were its higher operating speed and its steel construction, which allowed greater precision in the manufacture of the equipment and easier cleaning. Since the flats of the card moved continuously, the output per machine and per worker increased compared with the stationary carding machine. Moreover, the new card required less skill on the part of the operator than the stationary card. As a result of its labor-saving potential, the revolving flat card was adopted rapidly by the U.S. mills in the late nineteenth century.

When a fine yarn is desired, the cotton is next combed to remove any short fibers and create a sliver of long, parallel fibers. Slivers may be loosely twisted together to form "roving" at this stage. The combing machine has been less important in the history of the U.S. industry than improvements in other stages of textile production, because of the limited production of fine output in this country. The comber was invented in France in 1845. Its use in U.S. mills was infrequent until the twentieth century, and U.S. production of carding machines did not begin until 1897. Improvements in combers were based on the original French design, and the innovations brought higher speeds and increased productivity.

The slivers from either the carding or combing machines are next twisted in the fly frames, which draw the cotton in four successive frames. Drawing out produces a finer thread and also puts a twist into the cotton before it goes to the spinning process. Improvements in fly frames have focused on increasing their operating speed and improving the construction of the machines. In addition, product quality and production efficiency were improved by the application of "stop motions" on fly frames and other textile machinery, which stop the machines automatically when a thread breaks.

Advances in automation have led to the combining of the preparatory steps into one operation in the largest of today's mills. Direct-feed carding systems combine the opening, blending, and carding into one step and eliminate the picking stage altogether. The direct-feed carding system eliminates the need to transport the cotton between each stage. In 1985 about 10 percent of yarn output in the United States was produced by the new method.

The second stage in the textile process is spinning. Short staple fibers, such as cotton, must be tightly twisted together to form a firm thread of sufficient length for weaving into fabric. Early spinning methods used the distaff and the spindle. A length of cotton fiber from the distaff was attached to the spindle. The spinner whirled the spindle, which caused the fiber to be twisted, and then paused to wind the new thread on the spindle. Spinning occurred in two stages, requiring separate twisting and winding motions. Later the spinning wheel mechanized the process. Invented in India, the wheel soon spread to Europe and England in the Middle Ages. In addition to the improvement in speed, the spinning wheel produced a more uniform yarn by allowing the spinner to control the amount of twist given the fiber.

Three important British inventions improved spinning in the eighteenth century. James Hargreaves developed the spinning jenny in 1770, which introduced multiple spindles on the same frame. Sir Richard Arkwright developed a water-powered spinning machine that introduced the principle of continuous spinning by simultaneously twisting and winding the yarn on the spindle. The Arkwright water frame produced a stronger thread than the spinning jenny, which could be used for the "warp" yarns that form the lengthwise threads on looms. Samuel Crompton invented the mule spinning machine in 1779, which was patterned after the intermittent spinning process used by the spinning wheel and spinning jenny. The mule revolutionized spinning by raising the number of spindles that were operated by a single machine and allowing the mass production of spun yarn. The mule could be used for spinning fine as well as coarse yarns.

The mule is a complex machine that consists of spindles mounted on a carriage, which runs on a five-foot-long track. The mule operates on the ancient two-step spinning process. Yarn is drawn out as the carriage is pushed forward. When the carriage stops, the spindles begin to revolve and twist the threads. As the carriage returns, the yarn is wound on the spindles. The mule was operated by hand until the "self-acting" mule was introduced in 1830. Improvements in the mule during the nineteenth century increased its speed and the number of spindles placed on each machine.

A competing spinning process, ring spinning, was developed by an American in 1831 and was based on the continuous method of spinning first used in Arkwright's water frame. The ring consists of several stationary spindles fixed on a frame, and each spindle holds a bobbin upon which the yarn is wound. Around each spindle is a steel ring that is connected to a wire called a traveler. The traveler pulls the thread while putting a twist in it and is rotated by the ring, which moves slowly up and down the spindle to wind the twisted yarn on the bobbin. Thus, ring spinning operates at a much greater speed than the processes based on the two-step, intermittent spinning technique.

Ring spinning did not become prevalent in the United States until further improvements in the ring were made by American manufacturers in the 1870s, however. The Sawyer and Rabbeth ring spindles are often considered the first of the new generation of rings to become popular in U.S. mills, but a number of improvements in the speed and quality of ring spinning were introduced by American inventors and equipment manufacturers in the late nineteenth century.

At first, use of the ring was constrained by the type of yarn to be produced. High operating speeds that put stress on the thread prevented the spinning of thin, fine yarns on ring spindles. As a result, the mule's advantage in producing higher grades of yarn allowed that method to remain competitive with ring spinning, in spite of the higher operating speed and lower labor cost of ring spinning. Design advancements in the ring eventually permitted production of fine yarns, however, and mule spinning was phased out in the United States.

Saxonhouse and Wright (1983) point to complementary advancements made in drawing out the cotton fiber before it was fed to the ring spindle, which improved the handling of fragile threads. The Casablancas apparatus developed in the early twentieth century improved the process of drafting or pulling the thread by using elastic bands to increase the surface contact with the fibers, rather than simply drawing the thread through metal rollers as in the traditional method. The Casablancas system helped to extend the applications of ring spinning to fine yarns, which made mule spinning obsolete.

Ring spinning remains the dominant spinning technique in the United States, but new spinning processes are now being developed that are beginning to replace ring spinning in U.S. textile production. Already, 40 percent of the filling yarn (used to create the crosswise threads in woven goods) is produced by the open-end spinning method. The open-end method integrates the roving, spinning, and winding motions into one operation, and produces four times the output of ring spinning.

Air-jet spinning and friction spinning are promising inventions that are currently being developed for commercial use.

After spinning, the yarn moves to the next stage of production in preparation for weaving. It is important at this point to distinguish between two types of yarn: warp and weft (or filling). Warp yarn forms the lengthwise threads in a woven fabric, and weft, the crosswise threads. In the third stage of production, warp yarn is prepared for the loom by spooling, warping, and sizing the spun yarn. Yarn is unwound from the bobbins of the spinning machine to spools, which are moved to the warping machine. From there yarn is sized as it passes through a starch solution, and the treated yarn is then rewound and carried to the loom. Warp yarn is sized to strengthen the yarn, since weaving places greater stress on the warp than the weft yarns.

The weaving process involves the interlacing of yarns by using a loom to create a woven structure or fabric. First, the loom is prepared by drawing the warp threads to the frame of the loom. (This process was done by hand until the Barber Warp Tying Machine was introduced in 1904.) Next a shuttle filled with weft thread is wound from the bobbins prepared in the spinning stage. The process of weaving involves the separation of warp threads, "shedding," which creates a space through which the shuttle is passed. A length of thread from the shuttle, or "pick," is left by the shuttle, and that thread is pressed to the cloth already woven by "beating in" the pick. Although technological changes have increased the speed and quality of woven goods produced on looms, the weaving process still consists of these three basic motions: shedding, picking, and beating in.

Improvements in the weaving process began with the invention of the flying shuttle in England by John Kay in 1733. Whereas passing the shuttle through the shed had required two workers, one on each side of the loom, the flying shuttle device sent the shuttle flying through the shed by the efforts of just one worker. A series of inventions led to the development of the power loom, which significantly increased weaving speed. The first power-driven loom was invented by the Englishman Edmund Cartwright in 1785, and a series of improvements led to the introduction of the power loom to America in 1814. In 1837 a British machinist working in a U.S. mill developed a power loom that could weave fine goods, and hand looms were phased out of U.S. textile production.

The next significant advancement in loom design was the invention of the automatic loom. The type first introduced in America was the Northrop loom, which was marketed by the Draper Company. The advantages of the new loom were the automatic replacement of empty bobbins in the shuttle and stop motions that automatically stop the loom when a thread breaks. These inventions dramatically reduced labor costs by increasing the number of looms that one weaver could tend. A weaver was able to tend fourteen to thirty automatic looms compared to just six to eight plain looms in that period. The automatic loom was at first limited to weaving only coarse fabrics, but improvements gradually extended its use to a wider range of fabric grades and styles of weave.

Modern looms have been refined by increasing the number of weaving functions that are automated and by improving the quality of the fabric produced. The earlier mechanical methods have been supplemented by pneumatic suction, which has allowed the weaving of the most delicate fabrics on automatic looms. The newest looms are shuttleless. Shuttleless looms use a variety of techniques to thread weft yarn through the loom. The dummy shuttle method makes use of an empty shuttle that travels through the shed without weft, but leaves a trail of yarn behind it. Rapier looms carry weft by means of a rigid rod or flexible steel tape, which can be wound on a wheel to save floor space after it passes through the shed. Water-jet and air-jet looms propel a length of weft across the loom on a jet of water or air. The shuttleless looms have the advantages of operating at three times the speed of conventional looms, and at quieter noise levels. About one-third of U.S. woven output in 1985 was produced on the new shuttleless looms.

Woven fabrics require finishing treatment in the final stage of textile production. Before finishing, fabrics are "grey goods" and require extensive cleaning and mending when the cloth arrives from the weaving department. Cottons are frequently scoured and then bleached to remove the natural color of the fiber. Mercerization is applied to cotton fabrics to improve the luster, strength, and affinity for dyes. The process was invented and practiced in England in the mid–nineteenth century and became popular in the United States two decades later after improvements were made in the treatment. The fabric is also dried before final treatments are begun, since water is used in various stages of textile production.

To enhance the appearance of the cloth, various treatments may be applied, including brushing and other processes that use heat and special equipment to produce different surfaces on the cloth. The feel of the fabric may be improved by sizing or softening the cloth. Fabric may also be treated for shrinkage control, crease resistance, fire resistance, or waterproofing to improve its performance. Dyeing and printing are final treatments that add variety and appeal to the finished textile products.

As in the case of the previous stages of textile production, automation of the finishing machinery has improved the speed and quality of the final preparation of the textile fabrics. In particular, computerized testing devices have increased quality control and reduced testing time and cost in modernized mills. Advances in chemistry have been applied to the bleaching, dyeing, and other treatment of fabrics to improve the quality of the final product.

Bibliography

Backman, Jules, and M. R. Gainsbrugh. *Economics of the Cotton Textile Industry.* New York: National Industrial Conference Board, 1946.

Bacon, Kenneth H. "Shrinking Wage Gap Helping U.S. Firms." *Wall Street Journal,* 23 March 1987, 1.

Bailey, Martin Neil, and Alok K. Chakrabarti. "Innovation and U.S. Competitiveness." *The Brookings Review* 4 (Fall 1985): 14–21.

Bellante, Don. "The North-South Differential and the Migration of Heterogeneous Labor." *American Economic Review* 69 (March 1979): 166–75.

Betancourt, Roger R. and Christopher K. Clague. *Capital Utilization.* New York: Cambridge University Press, 1981.

Berglund, Abraham, George Talmage Starnes, and Frank Traver de Vyver. *Labor in the Industrial South.* Charlottesville: The Institute for Research in the Social Sciences, University of Virginia, 1930.

Bernstein, Irving. *The Lean Years: A History of the American Worker 1920–1933.* Boston: Houghton Mifflin, 1960.

Browne, Lynn E. "How Different Are Regional Wages? A Second Look." *New England Economic Review* (Federal Reserve Bank of Boston) (March–April 1984): 40–47.

Carlino, Gerald A. "Do Regional Wages Differ?" *Business Review* (Federal Reserve Bank of Philadelphia) (July–August 1986): 17–25.

Carlson, Leonard. "Labor Supply, the Acquisition of Skills and the Location of Southern Textiles Mills, 1880–1900." *Journal of Economic History* 41 (March 1981): 65–71.

Chacholiades, Miltiades. *International Trade Theory and Policy*. New York: McGraw-Hill, 1978.

Chen, Chen Han. "Regional Differences in Costs and Productivity in the American Cotton Manufacturing Industry, 1880–1900." *Quarterly Journal of Economics* 55 (August 1941):533–66.

Clendinen, Dudley. "Textile Mills Squeezed in Modernization Drive." *New York Times*, 26 October 1985, 8.

Coelho, Philip R. P., and Moheb A. Ghali. "The End of the North-South Wage Differential: Reply." *American Economic Review* 63 (September 1973): 757–62.

Copeland, Melvin. "Technical Development in Cotton Manufacturing Since 1860." *Quarterly Journal of Economics* 24 (November 1909): 109–59.

———.*The Cotton Manufacturing Industry in the United States*. Cambridge: Harvard University Press, 1912.

Cotton Textiles Committee. *A Study on Cotton Textiles*. Geneva: General Agreement on Tariffs and Trade, 1966.

Creamer, D., D. Dobrovolsky, and I. Borenstein. *Capital in Manufacturing and Mining, Its Formation and Financing*. Princeton: Princeton University Press, 1960.

Davis, Lance. "Capital Immobilities and Finance Capitalism: A Study of Economic Evolution in the United States 1820–1920." *Explorations in Economic History* 1 (Fall 1963): 88–105.

———."The Investment Market, 1870–1914: The Evolution of a National Market." *Journal of Economic History* 25 (September 1965): 355–99.

———."Capital Mobility and American Growth." In *Reinterpretation of American Economic History*, edited by R. Fogel and S. Engerman. New York: Harper and Row, 1971.

Doane, David P. "Regional Cost Differentials and Textile Location: A Statistical Analysis." *Explorations in Economic History* 9 (Fall 1971): 3–34.

Easterlin, Richard. "State Income Estimates." In *Population Redistribution and Economic Growth in the U.S. 1870–1950*, by Everett Lee et al., vol. 2. Philadelphia: The American Philosophical Society, 1957.

Feller, Irwin. "The Draper Loom in New England Textiles, 1894–1914: A Study of Diffusion of an Innovation." *Journal of Economic History* 26 (September 1966): 320–47.

———."The Draper Loom in New England Textiles: A Reply." *Journal of Economic History* 28 (December 1968): 628–30.

———."Production Isoquants and the Analysis of Technological and

Technical Change." *Quarterly Journal of Economics* 86 (1972): 154–61.

Fischbaum, Marvin N. "An Economic Analysis of the Southern Capture of the Cotton Textile Industry Proceeding to 1910." Ph.D. diss., Columbia University, 1965.

Galenson, Alice. "The Migration of the Cotton Textile Industry from New England to the South: 1880–1930." Ph.D. diss., Cornell University, 1975.

Gibb, George S. *The Saco-Lowell Shops: Textile Machinery Building in New England, 1813–1949.* Cambridge: Harvard University Press, 1950.

Hekman, John. "The Product Cycle and New England Textiles." *Quarterly Journal of Economics* 95 (June 1980): 697–717.

Hekman, John and John S. Strong. "The Evolution of New England Industry." *New England Economic Review* (Federal Reserve Bank of Boston) (March–April 1981):35–46.

Horowitz, Rose A. "Textile Imports Spin Sad Yarn for Jobs." *Journal of Commerce*, 5 September 1985, 1A.

James, John A. *Money and Capital Markets in Postbellum America.* Princeton: Princeton University Press, 1978.

Kennedy, Stephen J. *Profits and Losses in Textiles: Cotton Textile Financing Since the War.* New York: Harper and Brothers, 1936.

Kohn, August. *The Cotton Mills of South Carolina.* Columbia: South Carolina Department of Agriculture, Commerce and Immigration, 1907.

Kristof, Nicholas D. "Great Textile Trade Debate." *New York Times*, 23 July 1985, 29.

Lachica, Eduardo. "U.S. Curbs Growth in Textiles Shipped by Taiwan in Pact." *Wall Street Journal*, 15 July 1986, 26.

———. "U.S. Puts Curb of 0.8% on Growth of Korean Textiles." *Wall Street Journal*, 5 August 1986, 32.

Ladenson, Mark L. "The End of the North-South Wage Differential: Comment." *American Economic Review* 63 (September 1973): 754–56.

Lahne, Herbert J. *Labor in Twentieth Century America: The Cotton Mill Worker.* New York: Farrar and Finehart, Inc., 1944.

Lazonick, William. "Factor Costs and the Diffusion of Ring Spinning in Britain Prior to World War I." *Quarterly Journal of Economics* 96 (February 1981): 89–109.

———. "Rings and Mules in Britain: Reply." *Quarterly Journal of Economics* 99 (May 1984): 393–98.

Leamer, E. E. "Let's Take the Con Out of Econometrics." *American Economic Review* 73 (March 1983): 31–44.

Lemert, Benjamin F. *Cotton Textile Industry of the Southern Appalachian Piedmont*. Chapel Hill: University of North Carolina Press, 1933.

Lester, Richard. "Trends in Southern Wage Differentials Since 1890." *Southern Economic Journal* 11 (April 1945): 317–44.

McHugh, Cathy. "The Family Labor System in the Southern Cotton Textile Industry, 1880–1915." Ph.D. diss., Stanford University, 1981.

McKenzie, Richard B., with Steven D. Smith. "The Loss of Textile and Apparel Jobs: The Relative Importance of Imports and Productivity." Working paper no. 96. St. Louis: Center for the Study of American Business (January 1986).

McUsic, Molly. "U.S. Manufacturing: Any Cause for Alarm?" *New England Economic Review* (Federal Reserve Bank of Boston) (January–February 1987): 3–17.

Maddala, G. S. *Econometrics*. New York: McGraw-Hill, 1977.

———. *Limited-dependent and Qualitative Variables in Econometrics*. Cambridge: Cambridge University Press, 1983.

———. "Econometric Issues in the Empirical Analysis of Thrift Institutions' Insolvency and Failure." Invited working paper no. 56, Washington, D.C.: Office of Policy and Economic Research, Federal Home Loan Bank Board (October 1986).

Magee, Stephen P. *International Trade*. Reading, Mass.: Addison-Wesley, 1980.

Malabre, Alfred L., Jr. "Gap Between U.S., Foreign Wages Widens," *Wall Street Journal*, 17 July 1985, 6.

Mansfield, Edwin. "Wage Differentials in the Cotton Textile Industry, 1933–1952." *Review of Economics and Statistics* 37 (February 1955): 77–82.

Mitchell, Broadus. *The Rise of Cotton Mills in the South*. Baltimore: Johns Hopkins University Press, 1921.

Mitchell, Broadus, and George Sinclair Mitchell. *The Industrial Revolution in the South*. Baltimore: Johns Hopkins University Press, 1930.

Mitchell, Daniel J. B. "International Convergence with U.S. Wage Levels." Paper presented at the meetings of the Industrial Relations Research Association, San Francisco, December 1983.

Navin, Thomas. *The Whitin Machine Works Since 1831*. Cambridge: Harvard University Press, 1950.

Newman, Robert. "Industry Migration and Changing Regional Wage Patterns." Ph.D. diss., U.C.L.A., 1980.

Oates, Mary. *The Role of the Cotton Textile Industry in the Economic Development of the American Southeast: 1900–1940*. New York: Arno Press, 1975.

————. "Discussion (of Carlson 1981)." *Journal of Economic History* 41 (March 1981): 72–73.

Pindyck, R. S., and D. L. Rubinfeld. *Econometric Models and Economic Forecasts*. New York: McGraw-Hill, 1976.

Pine, Art. "U.S. Textile Pact Is Seen Increasing Rift in Congress on Overriding Veto of Quotas." *Wall Street Journal*, 4 August 1986, 2.

————. "U.S., Japan Set Growth Limits in Textile Trade." *Wall Street Journal*, 17 November 1986, 37.

Rook, James R. "Labor Skill Composition, Elasticities of Substitution and Industrial Migration." Ph.D. diss., North Carolina State at Raleigh, 1979.

Salmans, Sandra. "The Textile Industry Shakes Itself Up." *New York Times*, 10 May 1981, sec. 3., p. 1.

Samuelson, Paul. "International Trade and the Equalization of Factor Prices." *Economic Journal* 58 (June 1948): 163–84.

————. "Equalization by Trade of the Interest Rate Along with the Real Wage." In *Trade, Growth and The Balance of Payments*, edited by Robert E. Baldwin. Chicago: Rand McNally, 1965.

Sandberg, Lars. "American Rings and English Mules." *Quarterly Journal of Economics* 83 (February 1969): 25–43.

Saxonhouse, Gary, and Gavin Wright. "New Evidence on the Stubborn English Mule." University of Michigan, Ann Arbor. Mimeograph, 1983.

Schmidt, William E. "Textile Defends Its Last Bastion." *New York Times*, 23 June 1985., sec. 3, p. 4F.

Shen, T. Y. "A Quantitative Study of Production in the American Cotton Textile Industry, 1840–1940." Ph.D. diss., Yale University, 1956.

Shiells, Martha, and Gavin Wright. "Night Work as a Labor Market Phenomenon: Southern Textiles in the Interwar Period," *Explorations in Economic History*, 20 (October 1983): 331–50.

Smiley, Gene. "Interest Rate Movement in the United States 1888–1913." *Journal of Economic History* 35 (September 1975): 591–620.

Smith, T. R. *The Cotton Textile Industry of Fall River, Massachusetts*. New York: King's Crown Press, 1944.

Sokoloff, Kenneth L. "Investment in Fixed and Working Capital During Early Industrialization: Evidence from U.S. Manufacturing Firms." *Journal of Economic History* 44 (June 1984): 545–56.

Stanback, Thomas M., Jr. *Tax Changes and Modernization in the Textile Industry*. New York: Columbia University Press, 1969.

Stigler, George. *The Organization of Industry*. Homewood, Ill.: Richard D. Irwin, 1968.

Sylla, Richard. "Federal Policy, Banking Market Structure, and Capital Mobilization in the United States, 1863–1913." *Journal of Economic History* 29 (December 1969): 657–85.

"Textiles, Apparel & Home Furnishings." *Standard & Poor's Industry Surveys* (May 15, 1986): sec. T, 77–99.

United Nations Industrial Development Organization (UNIDO). Textile Industry, monograph no. 7. New York: United Nations, 1969.

United States Bureau of the Census. *Tenth Census*. Vol. 2, *Report on the Manufactures of the United States*. Washington, D.C.: Government Printing Office, 1883.

———. *Eleventh Census*. Vol. 2, *Manufacturing Industries*. Part I, "Totals for States and Industries." Washington, D.C.: Government Printing Office, 1895.

———. *Twelfth Census*. Vol. 1, *Population*. Washington, D.C.: Government Printing Office, 1902.

———. *Twelfth Census*. Vol. 8, *Manufactures—States and Territories*. Washington, D.C.: Government Printing Office, 1902.

———. *Manufactures, 1905*. Washington, D.C.: Government Printing Office, 1907–8.

———. *Thirteenth Census*. Vol. 1, *Population*. Washington, D.C.: Government Printing Office, 1913.

———. *Manufactures, 1914*. Washington, D.C.: Government Printing Office, 1918–19.

———. *Fourteenth Census*. Vol. 9, *Manufactures, 1919: Reports by States*. Washington, D.C.: Government Printing Office, 1923.

———. *Fifteenth Census*. Vol. 3, *Manufactures: Reports by States*. Washington, D.C.: Government Printing Office, 1933.

———. *Historical Statistics of the United States, Colonial Times to 1957*. Washington, D.C.: Government Printing Office, 1960.

United States Bureau of Labor Statistics. *History of Wages in the United States from Colonial Times to 1928*, bulletin no. 604. Washington, D.C.: Government Printing Office, 1934.

United States Department of Commerce. "Highlights of U.S. Export and Import Trade (FT990)." (December 1975): 112–13.

———. "Highlights of U.S. Export and Import Trade (FT990)." (December 1985): C(16–17).

———. "Textiles." *1986 U.S. Industrial Outlook* (January 1986): sec. 42, 1–6.

———. "Textiles." *1987 U.S. Industrial Outlook* (January 1987): sec. 41, 1–2.

Uttley, T. W. *Cotton Spinning and Manufacturing in the United States.* Manchester, Eng.: University of Manchester Press, 1905.

Vernon, Raymond. "International Investment and International Trade in the Product Cycle." *Quarterly Journal of Economics* 80 (1966): 190–207.

Williams, Linda, and Alix M. Freedman. "Bid by Burlington Industries to Buy Masland Accepted." *Wall Street Journal*, 17 June 1986, 20.

Wright, Gavin. "Cheap Labor and Southern Textiles, 1880–1930." *Quarterly Journal of Economics* 96 (November 1981): 605–29.

Index

About the Author

NANCY FRANCES KANE is an industry economist at First In-
terstate Bancorp, Los Angeles. She was formerly an Economist
at the Federal Reserve Bank of New York.